Consistency

How Being Consistent Can Guarantee Your Success

(The Key to Permanent Stress Relief Unleashing the Power of Consistency and Growth)

Richard Walker

Published By **Ryan Princeton**

Richard Walker

All Rights Reserved

Consistency: How Being Consistent Can Guarantee Your Success (The Key to Permanent Stress Relief Unleashing the Power of Consistency and Growth)

ISBN 978-1-7770663-4-5

No part of this guidebook shall be reproduced in any form without permission in writing from the publisher except in the case of brief quotations embodied in critical articles or reviews.

Legal & Disclaimer

The information contained in this book is not designed to replace or take the place of any form of medicine or professional medical advice. The information in this book has been provided for educational & entertainment purposes only.

The information contained in this book has been compiled from sources deemed reliable, and it is accurate to the best of the Author's knowledge; however, the Author cannot guarantee its accuracy and validity and cannot be held liable for any errors or omissions. Changes are periodically made to this book. You must consult your doctor or get professional medical advice before using any of the suggested remedies, techniques, or information in this book.

Upon using the information contained in this book, you agree to hold harmless the Author from and against any damages, costs, and expenses, including any legal fees potentially resulting from the application of any of the information provided by this guide. This disclaimer applies to any damages or injury caused by the use and application, whether directly or indirectly, of any advice or information presented, whether for breach of contract, tort, negligence, personal injury, criminal intent, or under any other cause of action.

You agree to accept all risks of using the information presented inside this book. You need to consult a professional medical practitioner in order to ensure you are both able and healthy enough to participate in this program.

Table Of Contents

Chapter 1: What Is Consistency? 1

Chapter 2: Why Does Constitency Matter? 7

Chapter 3: Reasons Why Consistency Is Not All Or Nothing. 16

Chapter 4: Small Steps That Produce Big Results 23

Chapter 5: How To Maintain Consistency 29

Chapter 6: How Do Consistency And Habits Interact? 36

Chapter 7: What Are The Benefits Of Consistency? 41

Chapter 8: How To Be Consistent Regardless... 45

Chapter 9: The Science Of Checklists 50

Chapter 10: Building Effective Checklists 60

Chapter 11: Tailoring Checklists For Different Domains................................. 74

Chapter 12: Checklist Implementation Strategies 83

Chapter 13: Checklist For Daily Life 99

Chapter 14: Troubleshooting And Optimizing Checklists 109

Chapter 15: Measuring The Impact Of Checklists 121

Chapter 16: Real World Examples Of Checklist Success 138

Chapter 17: What Is Consistency? 146

Chapter 18: Why Is Consistency Important? 152

Chapter 19: Why You Shouldn't Think Of Consistency As All Or Nothing 159

Chapter 20: How Little Actions Can Lead To Great Results 166

Chapter 21: How To Keep Being Consistent 171

Chapter 22: Habits And Consistency 177

Chapter 23: What Benefits Can
Consistency Provide You? 180

Chapter 1: What Is Consistency? `

Consistency is described as "conformity in the application of a few element, usually that it's required for the sake of commonplace feel, accuracy, or equity." That is the maximum complete definition of consistency.

When you have got a have a look at it that manner, it all seems very simple and easy to put into effect on your personal lifestyles. It seems to be easy to be consistent and virtually depend on and expand close to regular people, proper? But not so fast. It's now not as easy as you can undergo in mind.

There are a long way too many those who acquire as true with that being without a doubt normal can be clean. They be given as true with it is going to be easy to area this idea into effect and make it a everyday part of their lives. They persuade themselves, "I may be a constant character consequences, and as soon as I begin, I'll in no way prevent." But this is definitely now not the case.

Give Consistency Credit.

The truth is that not sufficient humans deliver consistency enough credit score rating. However, however being overlooked and underrated as a critical life technique, consistency has helped many people thrive and may do the identical for you.

So, precisely what's consistency? Not the older definition or hazy description. What does real fidelity in real lifestyles look and experience like? What is the prevent result? What are some real-lifestyles examples of consistency?

Let us start with what consistency is not. Being regular does not imply giving in or persisting in a function that is detrimental to you, your relationship, your profession, or others. It does now not mean that you need to follow antique rituals or mind inside the gift era. Because matters are changing masses faster in the international than they have in the beyond.

No, keeping continuity does no longer require refusing to adjust to converting activities. There are a ways too many people in the worldwide who are usually inconsistent in all the incorrect methods. Being regular does no longer provide you with permission to be harsh or hurtful to others, even in case you do not realize or understand them. That is not being constant or "actual to yourself," but as an alternative cruel.

Doing what continuously works necessitates consistency in each philosophy and exercise. It manner sticking to tried-and-actual techniques that get the challenge performed, no matter what the art work is. When what you're doing is working, there is no purpose to alternate definitely because of the fact the present day politician, enterprise multi-millionaire, or existence train says you should.

It's about lowering via the distractions and temptations of get-it-finished-quick plans and approaches and doing handiest what works and supplies the exceptional results time and time another time.

When you check a person's fulfillment in commercial enterprise agency, it isn't always typically due to the truth they have been looking to shake matters up, think outdoor the field, and do a little element in reality particular.

Most of the time, those billionaires and global-elegance professionals attain achievement with the useful resource of doing what works. They keep matters smooth, preserve their eyes at the prize, find out a way to gather what they need, and keep on with it. That is the definition of consistency. Throughout history, it has helped many people accumulate remarkable fulfillment.

Hold regular.

Consistency moreover consists of remaining dependable and everyday.

You ought to constantly exert strive if you need to look results. This applies to all elements of your life, on the side of your expert, non-public, and social lives. For example, if you're trying to get in shape, robotically going to the gymnasium 3 times in line with week is a long way maximum suitable to working out difficult each unmarried day and in the long run being exhausted.

Results will come in case you located in the paintings. There is not any keeping off that, period.

You are not typically doing things for distinct human beings, and that may be a essential problem of consistency. You might also every so often act usually best for yourself. Being right to yourself consists of many outstanding elements.

For example, it includes following a diet plan, looking after your frame, going to bed at a regular hour, persevering with collectively with your interests, staying in touch with and near to the human beings you like, and sometimes treating yourself. You will start to lead a better, greater exciting life even as you begin to be regular in this vicinity of your lifestyles and consistent with no longer outstanding others however moreover yourself.

What are some real strategies for introducing consistency into your life? Consider dropping some weight. Do you accept as true with you studied it's miles higher to consume healthily all of the time with occasional candy treats cautiously, resulting in slower however longer-lasting weight reduction, or to take pride in a chain of dramatic crash diets determined with the aid of way of binges?

Chapter 2: Why Does Constitency Matter?

What is it approximately consistency that makes it so important on your existence and enterprise enterprise? Actually, there are several motives at the back of this. When you have got a test consistency carefully, you could find out how it could advantage you in masses of regions of your existence.

Consistency can assist us reduce thru the noise in a world in which we need energy of thoughts and energy of mind to focus on what is vital to us. However, in case you want to assemble a properly designed dependency, you need to be disciplined. And this area keeps you from straying out of your course. This is the primary cause why consistency is so essential.

Life And Business Consistency.

Assume you are trying to establish a ultra-modern business company or internet presence. If this is the case, you'll need to be self-disciplined if you need to create a few element on the manner to thrive and persist for a long term.

Create a method to help you live focused, discover new fabric, write the item's outline and body, edit it, after which publish it. And you have to do it once more the subsequent week. This is useful to you, your writing, your competencies, and the goal marketplace you preference to obtain.

Would you watch a TV display that didn't air on a normal foundation? Would you buy a newspaper that wasn't introduced every day? Obviously now not.

This will not be easy. Nothing, however, that calls for energy of will, strength of will, and numerous effort is straightforward. You will see the consequences ultimately.

With some consistency, you may also sense better approximately your self. This is some other cause why you want to embody into your lifestyles.

If you constantly observe via for your commitments, you may have more self assurance in your self and others can have more faith in you.

Building the precise assignment you're operating on every day would probably make you enjoy greater assured and glad together with your goals. As a stop result, you could maintain to paintings hard, create extra, and gain greater fulfillment. To be consistent, it is not about the outcome or the cease line. The improvement you are making every time you assemble that one-of-a-kind project is what consistency is all about.

You can tour again in time and notice the manner you completed this morning, weeks in the beyond, or 3 weeks in the beyond. It is about the method and growth, no longer the outcomes. By analyzing your development, you may adjust your tempo, benefit a elegant experience of your property, and preserve a clean and specific approach.

You might also assemble your self-self guarantee and get more comfortable with purpose-placing through retaining song of your improvement.

All That Consistency Can Bring You.

Do you need to stand out inside the crowd? Be a reliable person. Do you want others to look at you? Be a reliable individual. Always be on time every day. You will certainly gain a following and relationships with essential human beings if you can set up your self as someone, writer, or businessperson who is reliable and ordinary.

Create some element on the way to be certainly really worth bringing up or promoting.

Create a few detail so one may be sincerely well well worth promoting or speaking about.

Not all of the content you located up will cross viral. Not each corporation task will draw the hobby and clients you want. Not all relationships have the functionality to last an entire life.

The only manner to benefit the take delivery of as authentic with and maintain the hobby of others is to always be there. Because over time, those small, simple movements will collect to have a big impact on you, your close to pals and family, the businesses you start, the manner you observe yourself within the worldwide, and masses of one-of-a-kind subjects.

There are severa motives why preserving our commitment to tough artwork also can assist us gain exceptional success in existence.

When you behave on a ordinary basis, you adopt the identical subjects nearly each day. When we fail to execute responsibilities for a day or and then fail to reap our cause, it is simple to recognize why this occurred. Consistency holds us chargeable for each motion we take.

If you are the only sporting out the duties required to gain your dreams, no person else is guilty. Because we're able to be missing one or workdays, we may need to alternate our activities and conduct so as to finish our plans.

Consistency in daily existence assists us in turning into greater sincere within the eyes of others. Preaching to others is simple, however embodying our requirements can be greater difficult. Individuals that "walk the communicate" are appeared as tremendously sincere and dependable via others. When others agree with in you, it boosts yourself belief and verifies that what you're doing is worthy. Other humans's faith in us boosts our self guarantee and gives us the inducement to keep going for walks towards all of our dreams.

In terms of receive as actual with, performing usually can raise our relevance and pork up our recognition, specifically in case you paintings in a enterprise agency or are a pacesetter in some ability. People need to art work with humans who've a established tune record of accomplishment because regular difficult work creates lengthy-term consequences. This must cause extra business enterprise opportunities with customers. Working tough and constantly may also have a large effect on whether you're promoted or live a rank-and-file employee within the office.

Self-Control is Essential.

Being steady can be hard as it calls for a number of power of will, and if one isn't used to retaining steady in a unmarried's sports activities, it could come to be a totally new addiction. Consistency in exercising encourages trouble, sharpens our attention, and heightens our consciousness of what desires to be done. It is probably difficult to triumph over antique conduct, however consistency in all that we do is needed if we need to do greater topics and revel in non-public improvement.

If you constantly exercising a modern capability for a while, you can decide whether or not it'll be a achievement or a failure. If acquiring consequences quick is your factor, you can save you doing something or surrender in case you don't see results right now away. If you have got the force to do matters on a normal basis, you may push through and evaluate whether or not or not they will achieve achievement or no longer.

For all you understand, a assignment can also additionally first-class need minimal adjustments to the method to be triumphant, and you may not realize till you live with it in advance than giving up.

Consistency could make the difference between fulfillment and failure in all we do in life. Being steady may be difficult, particularly if you have to perform the equal movements each day due to the reality it could seem dull and repetitive. It is impractical to anticipate brief consequences because of the truth preserving consistency calls for persistence.

When regular behavior want to be installation, people can be hesitant to exchange. It is not regularly too past due to begin being normal, especially if we need to improve ourselves and gain our desires years from now. Seek advise from others, alongside facet a life teach, to help you emerge as greater inexperienced because of the reality going it by myself may be difficult.

Chapter 3: Reasons Why Consistency Is Not All Or Nothing.

Regardless of the evidence and facts, many humans trust they'll be each top notch successes or terrible screw ups. There are many folks who do not apprehend what they have got performed, although it's miles super and splendid and really worth of glory and acclaim.

There also are others who agree with they've got completed greater than sufficient and do no longer want to hold, strive more difficult, or achieve some component greater.

This is a case of all or not anything thinking. It's the belief that it is either this or that, A or B, and now not some thing else in amongst. When you live a lifestyles that is all black and white questioning with out a gray, you are doing your self a big disservice and drastically restricting your functionality.

When trying to be ordinary, many humans adhere to black and white, all or not some thing wondering. Why is it this form of regular feature of humans seeking to add extra balance to their lives? It's not pretty easy, however it has some issue to do with the truth that it hurts to look yourself set up desires and then fall quick of them.

Always and Never.

This type of wondering can reason hundreds of problems, specially if you're trying to be everyday and dependable. Thinking in phrases of all or nothing has an effect at the manner you understand your self and others. This way of thinking commonly employs absolute terms which consist of "continuously" and "in no manner." "I'm in no way going to be steady all the time, so I need to not strive!" Many human beings tell themselves this as they endeavor to be more normal of their personal and expert life. Furthermore, many human beings are not able to peer terrific alternatives because there's certainly suitable or horrible, and now not the use of a in-amongst. It may additionally make it hard, if not not feasible, to apprehend solutions.

When you follow all or now not something wondering, you will revel in like a failure more frequently, and you may additionally have decrease self-esteem because when you are both a fulfillment or a failure - and nothing else - the percentages of seeming like a complete failure are plenty better.

You may also be a bargain much less ready to take risks in case you are an all or now not some thing attitude, for you to make it difficult to be regular on a ordinary foundation. You want to take pleasant chances so one can remodel your life and the manner you do things, which incorporates the strategies in which you will be constant, sincere, and reliable. You might also want to assume outdoor the field, take a look at with new topics, push your self, and blend topics up. But you cannot try this on a everyday foundation in case you suppose in phrases of all or not anything.

Also, you can discover it tough to forgive your self on a ordinary basis, that may be a chief reason why all or now not some thing thinking cannot be used at the same time as turning into a regular character. When you do now not meet the state-of-the-art requirements you have got set for yourself, you want to be patient with yourself. You have to persuade your self which you did now not do everything you desired, that you did now not reap your objectives sincerely, however that you tried, and that is some component to be glad with. That is reason for party. You cannot get once more on the pony and try again in case you cannot forgive your self. And that may be a important issue of turning into ordinary or challenge some thing else.

Yes, grace, self-forgiveness, and self-compassion are required whilst in search of to amplify yourself and emerge as a disturbing person. And questioning in phrases of all or now not something will not let you reap this.

When someone thinks on this style, they may best consider themselves as successful or failed in their existence pastimes. It's all black and white; it is each this or that. That is the middle of all or not anything thinking, and it can take you down a direction from which you cannot pass back.

It is a mission.

Let's face it: becoming ordinary can be tough. It will necessitate which you set a aim for your self and gather a imaginative and prescient of the version of yourself which you need to be. Then it's a matter quantity of following through and taking the specified actions to emerge as that individual. That is a large venture! That way you could no longer constantly be ideal.

You will make mistakes, fall brief, and have to compare, try over again, and modify your method to turning into regular. And in case you are an all or no longer whatever, black and white philosopher, you may continuously restriction yourself.

This way of questioning is awful while you're looking to be everyday, however it's also hard at the same time as you're looking to collect relationships with special human beings. You look into your very non-public worthiness as each proper or horrible. However, with this binary idea sample, you can begin to apprehend extraordinary human beings as well. As a forestall stop result, you could bypass harsh and unfair judgment on yourself and others. When you're so pessimistic, the arena can appear to be a totally bleak location, which can enhance your emotions of cynicism, despair, and fear.

You can also additionally preference consistency now not first-rate from yourself, however moreover from others. That method you can assume hundreds from others to your lifestyles. You would require dependability and dependability from them. However, as formerly said, doing so isn't constantly sincere. You are not on my own in making mistakes and falling short every so often. Others will no longer usually be capable of attain consistency in a unmarried day. It ought to require time, further to faux beginnings, revisions, and nerve-racking moments.

If you're all or not something, you'll now not permit the ones near you to try, fail, strive again, and subsequently succeed.

As you could bet, this may now not permit for consistency from you or others close to you.

The bottom line is that you'll advantage no longer a few aspect from suffering from all or no longer a few factor mentality. All it'll do is set up unreasonable standards for your self and others. It is a certain manner to restriction your self and assure that you may by no means change, and that the adjustments made by using others will not be correct enough for you.

As you can see, it want to be prevented - specially if you are striving to make a first-rate trade to your life, together with becoming extra sincere.

Chapter 4: Small Steps That Produce Big Results

As with maximum subjects, becoming a consistent character is a marathon, now not a dash.

You've probably heard that earlier than approximately wonderful subjects, however it's despite the fact that proper for consistency. If you want to emerge as a honest individual or run a dependable industrial organization, you can not assume to regulate your attitude on the arena, the manner you do commercial corporation, and how you supply yourself and live your lifestyles in a right away.

That is, of direction, an all or not some thing way of questioning. And, as formerly said, being in that thoughts-set will virtually slow you down or altogether prevent you from being regular.

The truth is that turning into a everyday individual can be hard at the start. You may additionally moreover persuade yourself which you had been a certain way your entire lifestyles and that it's going to take a huge amount of exchange to change that now.

Take Your Time.

Yes, there is probably a number of artwork involved, however right here's the factor: this artwork does now not have to be finished . It is viable over the years, slowly however regularly. As difficult as it may seem, becoming regular is an act of consistency. Instead of trying to go through a sea change and appreciably remodel your lifestyles , use the marathon analogy and start adjusting minor subjects proper here and there over time. Before you recognize it, your entire existence and the way you control your business company and personal affairs might be changed, and you will see which you in truth have grow to be the shape of character you constantly knew you may be - you honestly did no longer do it abruptly within the blink of an eye.

Small steps are what you require. What are a few easy moves you could take to emerge as and stay normal?

It's an brilliant idea to amplify a nighttime ritual that you may accomplish every day. That's constantly a pleasant location to begin. Why past due at night time time? Because placing too much stress on oneself inside the morning can be an excessive amount of. You have already got masses to do in the morning, so you must reputation on the night time.

Perhaps you are attempting to observe a ebook. Here's an fantastic first step you may take: Before going to mattress, I test 3 pages. Set aside 15 mins to examine those 3 pages, regardless of what. You will study your 3 pages regardless of what you've got finished during the day, while you need to evoke, or how exhausted you are. It's quality 3! That is some factor you may do fast! You will reap this each night time time.

It does now not even have to be a few thing as big as that.

Perhaps it's far as easy as making use of moisturizer on your ft earlier than going to bed. That's a easy movement you could take every night time time, right? It simplest takes a few seconds.

Whatever it is, you need to do it each night. This is the manner of setting up consistency. It is purposefully being normal and proving to your self that you are capable of doing so. You are demonstrating to yourself that you can accomplish consistency, even though it's miles with some factor minor. This can are to be had in accessible inside the destiny on the same time as you feel like you have bitten off extra than you may chunk. You'll appearance lower back on the ones modest steps and remember that you could do it.

Why? Because you have got had been given, and this can serve as evidence.

Compile the Minor Details.

The secret to becoming ordinary is to take all the minor things you do on a ordinary foundation and acquire them right into a tale you tell yourself. When you upload all of those small information collectively, you could see that you are definitely definitely regular. You have not cautioned your self, "I need to be at artwork 15 mins early every day, without fail." Instead, you spoke back, "I need to awaken five minutes earlier every day," then "I want to preserve a snack to artwork every day," and in the end "I need to start my vehicle ten minutes in advance."

These are all little levels and dreams that you can accomplish. When you add all of them collectively, you get an desired fulfillment.

As you can see, taking modest movements outcomes in huge outcomes. You sincerely want to figure out what your final dreams are and then determine out what modest measures you could take to get there. There can in no way be too many modest steps. When you located all of them collectively, they show a direction that in the end results within the character you need to be and the consistency you want to exhibit.

Chapter 5: How To Maintain Consistency

You've discovered a way to be everyday, however the most important issue is to stay constant. And that won't be as simple as you do not forget you studied.

In truth, if you start to be normal however then drop the ball and prevent, you will be squandering a while - in addition to the that of others.

The entire element of consistency is to be regular.

But how do you pass about doing that? How do you preserve going? How are you capable of avoid losing the ball? It's truly fairly clean, but it does require a few forethought and attempt. But it's far well surely really worth the attempt ultimately.

Here are a few sports and preserve in thoughts if you want to maintain your marvelous success.

Be Practical in Your Goals:

It can be tough to be regular in case you do now not apprehend what you need to do. Make smooth, sincere dreams which might be easy to track as a give up quit end result.

You need to start via sketching out your definition of consistency. Next, keep in mind the minor steps that want to be taken to gain that intention. As previously indicated, this will hold you normal and prevent your venture from turning into too big, overwhelming, or no longer feasible.

Use Reminders:

Because that is a new exercise, it's far critical to remind your self to study via. Make an try and area reminders on your apparel, in your home, at work, and at faculty. New duties and conversations are clean to miss, specially at the same time as seeking to trade up your regular. Put reminders in locations in which you'll see them so you'll recollect them at some point of the day.

No consider how hard you try to be steady, you may make mistakes sometimes. So, even in case you make mistakes, attempt to maintain going. Even in case you are absolutely properly-organized, you may make errors sometimes. As a end result, you want to base your plans on your mistakes. If you're making a mistake, attempt now not to berate yourself.

Things like those display up on a ordinary basis.

If you harm a promise, pass over a date, or need to reschedule on someone, you are not necessarily dropping consistency.

It is real that different factors can also come into play. Even at the same time as it is important to prepare for the ones outdoor affects and try and keep away from them, they will on occasion derail us.

If you need to, you have got an amazing way to be extra steady. As a cease result, you need to get ok sleep at night time. The common grownup want seven to 8 hours of sleep in line with night time time. Those who're still in college are expected to do a great deal greater. Allowing your frame time to get better will make it much less complex to preserve consistency the following day.

Even if you need to peer effects proper away, it will take time. It can be difficult to exchange your way of wondering, and you could not see instant consequences. It may be difficult to uproot your whole life and introduce a slew of new practices .

As a end result, you must supply your self a while to decide out what abilities incredible for you.

You must moreover be tenacious at the same time as keeping realistic. In popular, becoming a dependancy necessitates performing some issue regularly for spherical a month. Don't neglect to set minor dreams alongside the way. Try now not to tackle an excessive amount of right away. Minor tweaks will upload up over the years.

You'll additionally need to set obstacles to your intimate relationships and duties. These boundaries can also make it less difficult that permits you to keep your half of of the agreement because of your expectations of others. Setting the ones boundaries will make sure that you in no way tackle extra than you may cope with. For example, inform your enterprise that you do not need to paintings on weekends or at uncommon hours. You also can switch your mobile smartphone off altogether to tell your employees that you'll be unavailable inside the nights, weekends, or vacations.

If you exchange your way of questioning, you will be greater consistent.

Keep this in mind as you are trying to find to trade this form of big element of your existence.

Because we aren't machines, there will be days while we do not feel like doing some thing. For this purpose, we need to all lease motivational equipment. What need to you do in case you lack strain to finish your art work? Despite the truth that it can be tempting to desolate tract our dreams for the day, there are steps we are able to take to address this problem. If you're feeling down, torpid, weary, or unhappy, there are some strategies you can try and decorate your motivation.

Look After Yourself.

Making most effective commitments you could maintain is some different important dependancy to increase in case you need to be extra ordinary. People discover it impossible to withstand at the same time as they may be cherished by the usage of others. As a surrender end result, even as someone pleads for our help, all of us have a tendency to mention yes. While it is right to have the useful resource of others, it's far vital to keep away from making guarantees we cannot maintain. If you need to stay a extra regular life, you need to preserve your commitments. On the opportunity hand, it is easy to feel overworked, resulting in some obligations slipping thru the cracks.

Make an effort to indulge yourself in case you want to be greater constant.

After all, growing a ultra-modern dependancy is difficult. Make time-positive goals for your self. Then, as you purchased those goals, reward yourself. You can congratulate yourself on a challenge nicely finished in a whole lot of strategies.

It is critical to praise oneself or workout consistency because of the truth doing so reinforces wholesome behavior. Everyone has distinct approaches of profitable themselves. Never be scared to test with new mind, and recall to reward yourself whilst you got.

Chapter 6: How Do Consistency And Habits Interact?

Changing your conduct separately, step by step, is all it takes to come to be constant.

When expressed that way, it sounds far too simplistic and as even though it does no longer do enough honor to the oldsters that changed. But this is the critical cause of trying to emerge as more everyday. All you need to do is perceive the behaviors you need to alternate or contain into your routine and then pass after them.

Habits best ultimate good-bye until they emerge as 2d nature to you. When you start forcing your self to pursue the ones behavior, you may train yourself to do them continually and purpose them to a part of your personality, lifestyles, and habitual.

That is a crucial element of turning into everyday, but it is also a difficult thing. Making new behavior is hard, and maintaining oneself sincere and ordinary in repeating them is even extra hard. However, it's miles a vital step in case you need to be a consistent and dependable man or woman.

How to Break Bad Habits.

So, how can you broaden new conduct and lead them to part of your character?

It actually is that easy. To start, write a list of all of the techniques you need to behave and the numerous techniques in which you'll be steady. Perhaps you need to be extra activate in responding smartphone calls or emails. You might likely need to attain at paintings faster. Perhaps you need to go to the gym on a regular foundation. Maybe you would as an opportunity put together dinner at home than devour out.

Okay, so you understand what your dreams are and the manner you need your lifestyles to seem. The 2d step on this technique is to put in writing down the behavior as a manner to influence you to that region and help you acquire your desires. As previously stated, you may begin small and extend behavior for yourself.

If you want to enhance your cellular telephone name move again charge, you could make an effort to call a friend or member of the family at least as soon as in line with week, each week. If you desire to achieve at work in advance, you can start by doing so best once every week, however you may maintain to accomplish that each week. The equal holds actual for going to the health club or ingesting at home.

Habits are often subjects that form organically interior us without the help of outdoor stimuli. So forcing oneself to make some may also furthermore sound everyday. But hold in thoughts what you can benefit if you enforce the ones practices into your life. This is the most effective method to "educate" yourself the manner to perform these duties and to do them on a everyday basis.

As you can see, this could bring about the development of latest factors of your character. This can transform you into someone who responds cellular telephone calls and emails, gets to paintings on time, chefs at home, and does some of different topics. But it's going to no longer be clean. You may moreover need to discover that you have some internal resistance to venture these gadgets. This won't revel in natural or traditional to you; it can feel pressured or ugly.

However, this may not commonly be the case. This is the way you extend behaviors so as to ultimately become 2d nature. Yes, it could not feel clearly natural in the beginning, however the extra you do it, the extra you exercising those new conduct, and the more you push your very own butt to do those gadgets, the less complex it becomes.

It's without a doubt in reality a depend of having commenced out and pushing your self to carry out those devices before the entirety.

It will all become clean when you make that first go with the flow, while you get started out.

You must keep in thoughts that being inconsistent is a dependancy that need to be damaged. If you are studying this ebook, you are probable prepared to become a dependable and sincere man or woman. You're bored with disappointing others, and you don't need to be that man or woman. That is why you are trying to overcome the vintage behaviors that have lead you so far, those which have made you unreliable and inconsistent.

It is ability; all it takes is time and tough paintings. But hard try is type of continually worthwhile, especially whilst it results in you being the character you aspire to be and apprehend you are capable of turning into.

Chapter 7: What Are The Benefits Of Consistency?

The outstanding technique to determine what consistency also can provide for you is to invite yourself: how do you enjoy about steady people and ordinary groups?

What consists of mind whilst you think about a person reliable and straightforward, a person who's constantly on time and continually can offer what they promise, and who is in no manner reminded or pressured to do things?

What are your thoughts about this character or industrial agency enterprise? Is it high quality or terrible? Is this a person you want to collaborate with frequently or someone you want to avoid?

We can presume which you price someone who's professional at their paintings, constant, and dependable. And that is the form of affect humans should likely have of you in case you artwork hard to turn out to be steady.

If you work difficult to remain everyday, you may create a lifestyles entire of healthful, sturdy relationships, strong business company connections, possibilities, exciting activities, and a serene and laid decrease back temper within the whole lot.

Change Your "YOU" Point of View.

The most essential issue that consistency can offer you with is the manner humans recognize you, their critiques of you, and their willingness to be with you and art work along you.

No one desires to paintings with or be close to a person who will continuously drop the ball and allow them to down. How frequently do you pay attention humans speak kindly approximately folks that are erratic and untrustworthy? Not very frequently. It's one of the worst tendencies a person need to have, and it can ultimately ruin relationships. It can depart you with few buddies and no destiny industrial enterprise opportunities.

You are announcing some factor whilst you are ordinary and reliable.

You are simply expressing trouble. You are indicating that you listen to others, recognize their emotions, and respect them. You are indicating that their time is treasured and that you do not take them, their time, or their availability as a right. And it says hundreds! That demonstrates which you are a loving, right, and sympathetic man or woman. That is the type of character with whom others preference to be buddies.

When you're inconsistent, you are declaring the exact opposite.

You are implying that you are aware that someone is preoccupied or that they've requested something of you and also you genuinely do now not care. You'll do it whilst you get to it, you could arrive while you want to, and you may do the whole thing at your private pace. This isn't always a person who makes concessions, listens to others, or simply cares approximately their sentiments.

Your behaviors communicate hundreds about you. Your movements exhibit to the arena the form of man or woman you're and the beliefs you preserve steeply-priced. If you strive tough to live normal, you will be rewarded with near friendships and first rate regard from others.

But hold one issue in mind: it isn't always consistency for you to supply you the ones benefits. You are the only who will. You might be giving these gives to yourself due to your difficult artwork, making plans, and willpower. The blessings of consistency are severa and may be existence-changing. They may additionally moreover want to suggest the distinction among making a chum and now not, or amongst getting a manner and now not. However, they'll be not provided to you. You have earned them.

Chapter 8: How To Be Consistent Regardless

Some people may also declare that they are constantly late, that they by no means get a few aspect finished on time, or that they most effective paintings at their very personal pace and cannot be counseled what to do. They declare that they cannot be contained. They remember they can not do subjects the manner others do.

These folks are effectively keeping that irrespective of how tough they may be attempting, they will by no means be consistent. It's now not in their blood, it's now not who they may be. It is not a few detail they'll be familiar with.

These people are, to vicinity it mildly, full of it. They have to not be listened to, nor need to they be believed.

And if you are this sort of humans, you need to clearly rethink the way you see yourself and offer yourself more religion because of the truth, no matter what you receive as proper with or who you're, you are able to being regular, reliable, and dependable. You may be the one who arrives on time, responds cell telephone calls, completes schoolwork on time, and follows through on ensures. You can reap this no matter your records, reviews, or individual.

It all comes proper right down to pushing yourself. Yes, a few people discover it much less difficult to be normal. This is due to the way they had been reared, the roles they have held, or only a few individual characteristics that don't revel in taught or analyze. But to mention you cannot be regular is ridiculous and unfaithful.

The reality is that everybody may be normal; they sincerely need to parent out what's keeping them lower decrease returned and what the nice technique is to converting that and avoiding the potholes and bottlenecks which could slow them proper all of the manner down to being dependable.

That is why we emphasised the want of keeping off all or not anything questioning and setting a method in region similarly to developing new behaviors. Work is needed! It's now not commonly clean! You can't wake up within the future and determine to be regular from then on. Instead, you may want to sit down, make a way, and genuinely check and consider the subjects which have previously averted you from doing this.

You can be regular no matter who you're. You can learn how to play the piano regardless of who you're. It may be tough at the manner to discover ways to play the piano proper now. You might also have only ever played one device in your life, have hassle memorizing topics, and don't have any herbal experience of rhythm. There may be many elements on foot towards you, and you can enjoy beaten certainly considering gambling the piano. But it's far possible; you'll actually must installation more try than someone who has grown up playing specific devices.

If honestly everyone, consisting of yourself, argues that consistency is surely too tough, they may be mendacity. Or, greater correctly, they may be underestimating themselves. They are settling for an lousy lot much less than they're capable of.

You must believe in your self. You need to simply accept as right with in yourself.

You need to reassure yourself that, even as consistency may be difficult, it's going to probably be nicely nicely really worth it on the identical time as you spot what it is able to do for you, your existence, your relationships, your assignment, and your destiny. It can be well well worth the attempt.

Doing hard obligations have to now not be frightening. And performing hard matters ought to no longer be prevented. Instead, performing hard matters should be advocated and everyday as it demonstrates your electricity, willpower, and strength.

No, it isn't smooth to end up everyday, but you may reap it via approach of making a technique, converting your thoughts-set, and pushing your self to make bigger new conduct that turn out to be 2d nature. The ultimate issue you want to do is surrender desire and promote yourself short.

You have large functionality. Everyone does. All you want to do is get started out out, bear in mind in yourself, and no longer give up.

Chapter 9: The Science Of Checklists

Fashions of industries, which include aviation, healthcare, venture manipulate, and everyday obligations have placed checklists to be immensely useful. Despite checklists' seeming simplicity, their performance is based mostly on cognitive and intellectual mind that control conduct and selection-making in human beings.

Working reminiscence is an critical cognitive aspect that underpins tick list efficacy. Working reminiscence, on occasion referred to as the "intellectual scratchpad," is the place of our reminiscence that quick stores and organizes data on the identical time as we're specializing in a venture. Although working memory has a finite functionality, it may come to be crushed and motive cognitive overload, mistakes, and forgetfulness. By giving the duties to be completed a written or seen illustration, checklists help in relieving a part of the cognitive load from running reminiscence. As a end result, there may be a decrease hazard of mistakes or omissions due to the reality that human beings may additionally deal with carrying out obligations in area of looking for to take into account them.

Checklists additionally benefit from the attention and attention mental concept. We regularly conflict with multitasking and distractions for the reason that our attention is a confined beneficial resource. Checklists may also additionally help us live on route and reputation at the important responsibilities, ensuring that no vital steps are overlooked. Checklists facilitate a success mission prioritization and attention allocation by using giving human beings a clean and ordered framework, which enhances usual overall performance and produces better outcomes.

Memory consolidation is a critical cognitive belongings that impacts how powerful checklists are. Memory consolidation is the transfer of statistics from short-time period reminiscence to prolonged-time period reminiscence for longer-term archiving. By operating closer to and repeating the fabric, checklists help with memory consolidation. The responsibilities and techniques are bolstered even as we use checklists regularly, which makes them extra remembered and less probably to be forgotten. This is particularly vital in challenging or annoying times whilst reminiscence lapses can also additionally have horrible consequences, which consist of in complicated scientific strategies or situations requiring essential selections.

The psychology concept of cognitive schemas, frequently referred to as highbrow fashions, is likewise used by checklists. Cognitive schemas are intellectual systems that accelerate the employer and processing of information. Task encoding, retrieval, and execution are made less difficult with the useful resource of checklists' prepared, recognizable nature, which fits with our cognitive schemas. People might also take in records more effectively by means of way of the usage of their premodern intellectual fashions and cognitive frameworks when they adhere to a familiar tick list style, which lowers cognitive load and aids in choice-making.

The highbrow idea of social effect and responsibility is every other psychological precept that checklists hire. A commonplace records of the obligations and obligations is created while checklists are applied in a set or organizational environment, encouraging obligation and cooperation. Checklists can be utilized by crew people to double-take a look at every superb's artwork, provide feedback, and make sure defined techniques are being observed. As a stop end result, average typical performance and safety growth due to the lifestyle of cooperation and watchfulness this is fostered.

Additionally, checklists hire the mental concept of addiction constructing. Automatic moves which may be due to positive signs and symptoms or stimuli are referred to as conduct. People who often use checklists as a routine or workflow might make bigger a addiction of doing so, making using them a natural and instinctive detail of their preference-making and assignment execution techniques. Because behavior are strong and prolonged-lasting, as quickly as someone has evolved one for the usage of checklists, they're much more likely to keep doing so, at the way to result in in addition improvements in trendy overall performance and outcomes.

Ultimately, the simplicity or usefulness of checklists is definitely one element in determining their efficacy; special elements encompass the cognitive and mental thoughts that underlie human conduct and selection-making. Utilizing the competencies of operating reminiscence, interest, reminiscence consolidation, cognitive schemas, social pressure, duty, and addiction improvement, checklists may additionally growth performance, reduce errors, and

How Checklists Enhance Decision Making, Memory, And Attention

The use of checklists extends past simple method control and crowning glory monitoring. They sincerely have a massive have an effect on on reminiscence, hobby, and preference-making, which makes them an powerful device for enhancing traditional overall performance and consequences throughout an entire lot of disciplines.

Making picks includes weighing possibilities, taking into account capacity repercussions, and attractive in a complicated cognitive system. However, some of cognitive biases, which includes overconfidence bias, anchoring bias, and affirmation bias, may also have an effect on desire-making and bring about lots less than wonderful alternatives. To help humans conquer prejudices and make better knowledgeable and affordable judgments, checklists provide an organized and methodical method to selection-making.

By supplying a thorough and nicely-organized listing of important elements, checklists may assist in choice-making. Critical questions, requirements, or elements that want to be taken beneath attention earlier than creating a desire is probably included in selection-making checklists. When using a checklist, humans are compelled to suppose seriously and punctiliously examine all pertinent elements, making sure that no critical facts or viewpoint is ignored. By decreasing the risk of biased or impulsive judgments, this could result in extra properly-knowledgeable and balanced conclusions.

Particularly underneath difficult or annoying activities, checklists useful beneficial resource in standardizing choice-making approaches. Due to time constraints, statistics overload, and emotional concerns, choice-making below those times may be hard. Checklists provide a specific and regular structure for choice-making, making sure that each one required techniques are taken and critical data is taken under consideration. This might also lessen the cognitive burden involved in making choices, allowing humans to make alternatives which are extra logical and nicely-based totally.

Additionally, checklists may additionally decorate reminiscence, an critical cognitive feature that includes encoding, storing, and retrieving facts. In loads of industries, from healthcare to aviation, memory issues can also have primary repercussions, in conjunction with lacking critical records or incorrectly remembering it. The sports activities, techniques, or statistics that must be recalled are represented in writing or visually thru checklists, which help in reminiscence encoding.

A checklist externalizes records, freeing up jogging reminiscence area and lowering the possibility of cognitive overload. By providing a honest supply of facts that is straightforward to evaluate and pass again to as critical, checklists can useful resource reminiscence healing. Recalling critical understanding can be made greater correct and with fewer mistakes as a result, enhancing fundamental performance and results.

Additionally, checklists might also moreover enhance hobby, an critical cognitive feature that includes that specialize in pertinent information and sifting thru distractions. Today's rapid-moving, information-rich worldwide frequently causes hobby to be break up, and distractions can also bring about errors or oversights. By offering a exceptional and nicely-organized framework for sports to be finished, checklists useful useful useful resource in directing interest.

Individuals can also moreover moreover prioritize paintings, reputation their hobby effectively, and stay targeted with the resource of the use of a checklist. In addition to appearing as reminders or signals, checklists moreover inspire human beings to stay on the proper tune and finish artwork in an orderly style. In tough or excessive-strain times while interest is critical, this may enhance interest, reduce down on errors, and enhance normal common overall performance.

Finally, checklists have a large impact on choice-making, reminiscence, and interest in addition to being clean gadgets for undertaking control. Checklists help to improve choice-making through supplying an prepared and methodical technique, eliminating biases, standardizing techniques, and encouraging vital thinking. Additionally, checklists help with reminiscence encoding and retrieval, decreasing the opportunity of reminiscence screw ups and mistakes. Checklists additionally increase concentration through the usage of using directing hobby and minimizing distractions. Therefore, using checklists in some of disciplines lets in beautify cognitive strategies, which in turn improves basic overall performance and outcomes.

Chapter 10: Building Effective Checklists

Whether its miles at artwork, at home, or on non-public duties, project manage is an critical ability for fulfillment in any attempt. It's clean to become beaten thru the sheer amount of exertions that should be completed due to the complexity and dreams of contemporary existence's ever-growing wishes.

Checklists may be without a doubt useful equipment in this situation to preserve us centered, prepared, and efficient. There are positive jobs which might be extra proper for checklists than others, and understanding which of them to apply is critical to maximizing the potential of inexperienced mission control. The following are key factors to recollect while identifying responsibilities which is probably high-quality acceptable for checklists.

Repetitive or Routine Tasks:

For jobs which may be repetitive or regular in nature, checklists are especially beneficial. A tick list can be used as a reminder of the techniques involved in those jobs, ensuring that not some thing is forgotten. These obligations regularly consist of a chain of moves that need to be located continually. For a multi-step manufacturing device, a software program installation technique, or a every day or weekly cleaning time desk, for instance, a checklist might be beneficial. By utilising a checklist, people can make sure that everything is finished within the proper series and no longer some thing is neglected, growing accuracy and performance.

Complex or Multi-Step Tasks:

Checklists may also be useful for complex or multi-step responsibilities. Complex jobs may be intimidating, making it easy to overlook essential techniques and purpose mistakes or delays. A tick list allows simplify hard jobs into smaller, extra plausible levels, making it less tough to comply with the procedure and quit each step in a methodical way. A checklist is probably useful for a venture manage method with many ranges, a clinical remedy with numerous steps, or a recipe with severa additives and education techniques, for example. Individuals also can decrease the possibility of mistakes or omissions thru using a checklist to make certain all required strategies are done.

High-Stress or Time-Sensitive Tasks:

Tasks which might be completed under excessive-pressure or time-sensitive situations can appreciably benefit from checklists. In such conditions, stress or time stress can impair cognitive function, important to errors or oversights. A tick list can function a reliable reference aspect that people can rely on, even under worrying or time-touchy situations. For instance, a tick list may be useful for emergency approaches, critical selection-making techniques, or time-touchy ultimate dates. By the use of a tick list, humans can make sure that crucial steps aren't skipped, even beneath excessive-stress or time-touchy conditions.

Safety-Critical or Compliance-Driven Tasks:

Checklists are very beneficial for duties that include safety-touchy or compliance-driven criteria. In many industries, which include manufacturing, aviation, and healthcare, compliance with guidelines, protocols, or protection measures is critical. A tick list can be used as a tool to make certain all relevant conditions are finished, reducing the opportunity of compliance mistakes or safety breaches. For a affected character safety protocol, pre-flight protection inspection, or splendid control technique, a checklist may be useful. The danger of errors or non-compliance is decreased while humans use a checklist to make sure that each one compliance necessities are glad.

Tasks with High Consequences of Error:

Checklists can be very useful for obligations that have a immoderate danger of mistake or failure. Such jobs have a excessive hazard of mistakes or failure, which might likely bring about crucial repercussions collectively with financial loss, reputational damage, or safety troubles. By supplying an prepared and methodical technique to artwork finishing touch, a tick list may also furthermore act as a protect in the direction of mistakes or disasters. A tick list, for instance, may be beneficial in advance than a surgical treatment, a financial audit, or the deployment of crucial software program program. People may also additionally additionally lower the opportunity of errors or failures by using the usage of the use of the use of a tick list to make sure all important strategies are completed.

Choosing the right sports for checklists is critical for efficient undertaking manipulate, to sum up. Tasks that are repetitive or recurring, problematic or multi-step, high-pressure or time-touchy, safety-critical or compliance-pushed, or with a immoderate possibility of mistake are all first-class candidates for checklists. When the usage of checklists for those kinds of sports activities, humans also can enhance their judgment, memory, and consciousness, so as to boom their accuracy, performance, and effectiveness. The risk of errors, oversights, or non-compliance is reduced even as all required strategies are completed typically and methodically way to checklists. Utilizing the electricity of checklists may also appreciably beautify process manipulate and increase common standard performance throughout pretty a number of contexts, which encompass the employer, the residence, and personal tasks. In order to live prepared, focused, and on route to perform your objectives, the subsequent time you're confronted with a hard project, keep in mind putting in a tick list. You can also moreover unharness the entire ability of green task control and characteristic your self for fulfillment with the proper assignments and a properly-designed tick list.

Structuring Checklists For Maximum Effectiveness

Our capability to execute subjects successfully, efficaciously, and usually may be significantly improved through the usage of the usage of checklists, which is probably effective equipment. But now not all checklists are made similarly. The way a tick list is prepared will typically determine how a success it's miles. The following are key standards for structuring checklists for maximum effectiveness, imparting a roadmap for organized and green challenge manipulate.

Clear and Concise:

Making and making sure that checklists are easy and succinct is the number one rule of first rate checklist shape. The guidelines and factors for each pastime or item on a checklist ought to be easy to apprehend and clean to comply with. Avoid the usage of abbreviations, acronyms, or technical terms that the customer may not be acquainted with. So that everyone can understand the tick list's content material cloth material, keep the wording smooth and number one. The character have to now not be overloaded with facts, therefore conciseness is also important. Each get admission to at the checklist needs to be succinct and without delay-beforehand, concentrating at the critical obligations or strategies needed to complete the entire work.

Logical and Sequential:

Making and making sure that checklists are logical and sequential is the second one rule of appropriate tick list shape. The association of the items on a tick list want to make enjoy and correspond to the venture's or device's herbal go with the glide or collection. Users can study the tick list glaringly and complete each mission or step in the right series manner to this. Structure the tick list based totally on the best and inexperienced manner to finish the duties or techniques. Prevent haphazard or arbitrary layouts that might throw the client off and reason mistakes or omissions.

Comprehensive and Specific:

Making and making sure that checklists are thorough and unique is the 1/3 rule of authentic tick list layout. Checklists must encompass all stages or responsibilities that want to be completed so as to finish the overall challenge or technique. Avoid the use of ambiguous or preferred language that could bring about interpretation or ambiguity. As an opportunity, be particular and thorough approximately every interest or manner, along with any pertinent facts, measurements, or completion dates. This reduces the possibility of errors or oversights on the identical time as furthermore supporting clients in having a smooth know-how of what desires to be finished.

Visual and Organized:

Making and ensuring that checklists are visually appealing and properly-prepared is the fourth rule of accurate tick list format. The shape, typeface, and formatting of a tick list want to be clear and it ought to be simple to apprehend. To make the tick list visually readable and scannable, use bullet elements, numbers, or checkboxes. To emphasize key facts or closing dates, do not forget the usage of coloration coding or highlighting. Users can also extra with out problem recognize the tick list's content and glide thru it with the useful aid of visual components.

Flexible and Adaptable:

Having flexible and adaptive checklists is the fifth rule of awesome tick list design. In order to account for any changes or versions in the pastime or device, checklists need to be created. Depending on the specifics of the situation or the desires, obligations or techniques ought to want to be delivered, modified, or removed. Make positive the tick list may be with out problems updated or modified as vital without losing its usefulness. To report any special instructions or grievance, think about permitting region for further notes or feedback.

Test and Refine:

Testing and improving checklists is the ultimate rule for growing green ones. Once a checklist has been organized, it's miles essential to check it in real situations and get consumer comments. To increase the usefulness of the checklist, pinpoint any regions in which customers also can want to struggle or run into problems. The tick list need to continually be advanced so you can live useful, powerful, and inexperienced over the years.

In order to create checklists which can be as successful as feasible, they want to be dependent, bendy, clean, succinct, logical, sequential, entire, and unique. These important guidelines will help you increase splendid checklists.

Incorporating Feedback Loops And Updates

The use of checklists can also furthermore considerably decorate performance, ensure correctness, and enhance artwork control. However, a checklist's usefulness should be continuously improved upon and optimized; it cannot be finished in a unmarried step. To make sure that your checklists are as effective as viable, you should embody remarks loops and updates.

Through using feedback loops, the checklist's customers may additionally moreover offer comments, insights, and mind. Feedback may additionally moreover come from pretty a few human beings, along side customers, give up customers, organization human beings, and supervisors. It detects any troubles or troubles and indicates regions that want improvement at the same time as moreover giving useful data on how the tick list is acting in workout. Observations, debates, and actual-time feedback are all examples of casual feedback loops. Formal comments loops consist of factors like questionnaires and assessments.

You may additionally get personal records of your checklist's fulfillment by way of which includes comments loops into your tick list technique. You might also use it to find any gaps, inconsistencies, or places that want development that have been no longer proper away apparent even as the tick list became being created. User comments also can offer insightful viewpoints and sensible software of the checklist, highlighting any troubles or barriers that could restrict its usefulness. Furthermore, it gives a danger to record fulfillment reminiscences or outstanding practices that can be disseminated to assist others perform better.

When feedback is received, it's miles vital to utilize it to inform tick list updates and enhancements. The checklist also can want to be up to date with the useful resource of being revised, modified, or progressed in response to go into. It could also encompass introducing new responsibilities, disposing of superfluous ones, or improving descriptions or commands. The checklist is being often stepped forward and optimized to make it greater beneficial, powerful, and man or woman-best.

It's vital to reflect onconsideration on replace frequency and discover a stability among balance and versatility. A tick list that receives too many modifications is probably complex and disturb the method, even as one which receives too few updates can also want to become stale and lots less useful. The nature of the activity or way, the complexity of the tick list, and the accessibility of remarks also can all have an impact on how regularly updates are made. In order to keep the checklist cutting-edge and steady with the converting requirements of the device or approach, it have to be often reviewed and updated primarily based totally on input.

It's critical to promote a way of lifestyles of non-stop development within the crew or organisation that employs the checklist similarly to comments loops. Encourage organization members to particular their reviews, thoughts, and pointers for adjustments primarily based mostly on their very very own reviews.

Chapter 11: Tailoring Checklists For Different Domains

Checklists are sturdy gear which have confirmed success in raising general overall performance, minimizing errors, and enhancing universal overall performance in quite a few sectors. Checklists were significantly accompanied and integrated into numerous sectors, from healthcare to aviation, finance to assignment manipulate, to expedite methods and guarantee that activities are done correctly and correctly.

Checklists have become crucial in loads of industries, which includes healthcare. In healthcare environments, proper medical procedures and affected person safety are paramount, and the usage of checklists may moreover drastically lessen mistakes and beautify affected character effects. To make certain that each one required methods are found in advance than, during, and after a surgery, surgical checklists, as an example, have been drastically utilized in strolling rooms. Checking for hypersensitive reactions or probably troubles is one of the factors on the ones checklists, at the thing of confirming the affected man or woman's identity and the surgery website online. Healthcare professionals may moreover increase affected person protection, reduce down on headaches, and reduce surgical errors with the beneficial resource of adopting surgical checklists.

In order to ensure constant and effective operations, checklists are also crucial inside the aviation business enterprise. For pre-flight preparations, in-flight strategies, and put up-flight inspections, pilots and flight crews depend on checklists. Pre-flight inspections, emergency protocols, conversation protocols, and one of a kind sports activities activities are all covered through those checklists. The use of checklists in aviation permits pilots and different company people study SOPs, lessen human mistakes, and guarantee the protection of each passengers and team.

Risk control, cutting-edge financial transactions, and regulatory compliance are all a part of the finance vicinity. In order to assure precision, uniformity, and conformity across severa techniques, checklists are employed in finance. Financial institutions, as an instance, hire checklists for regulatory compliance tests, threat evaluation, and the compilation of financial statements. Checklists assist monetary experts in adhering to described protocols, confirming the correctness of information, and decreasing dangers related to financial operations.

Checklists are often utilized in mission control as properly to assure proper challenge execution. Checklists are utilized by mission managers to time table, music, and manage distinct task sports activities and milestones. An object in a mission tick list can be "define assignment dreams," "create assignment agenda," "assign obligation," or "conduct first-rate assessments." Project managers can also make sure that each step is finished, that deadlines are fulfilled, and that deliverables are completed on time desk and inside price variety thru the usage of venture checklists.

The use of checklists in these and other areas shows how bendy and a achievement they may be in improving ordinary performance and minimizing mistakes. Checklists offer a methodical technique to difficult jobs, making sure that all required procedures are taken and essential particulars aren't overlooked. Additionally, they'll be superb schooling and onboarding tools that make it a great deal much less difficult for brand spanking new hires to choose up on and feature a study protocol fast. Since checklists are effectively adaptable to the nice requirements of many professions, they'll be useful at some point of a giant range of groups.

It's important to maintain in mind, but, that the layout, use, and non-prevent updating of checklists determines their efficacy. The format of checklists is critical, and that they want to embody clean and clean instructions. Checklists must additionally be constantly evaluated and updated relying on feedback and changes in the challenge or company desires. To ensure that checklists are used as it ought to be and constantly, it's also crucial to provide right education and education on their utilization.

Ultimately, checklists are powerful gadget that have a large sort of programs in severa industries, collectively with challenge manage, healthcare, aviation, and finance, among others. They beneficial beneficial aid in better outcomes, better performance, and less errors. Checklists offer a methodical technique to sports activities sports, useful resource in standardizing practices, and assure essential techniques aren't skipped. Achieving improved stages of accuracy, performance, and operational success is possible for agencies with the aid of the use of nicely-designed checklists for the duration of an entire lot of sectors.

Customizing Checklists For Specific Industries, Professions, Or Personal Goals

In order to meet the particular wishes and specifications of numerous sectors, professions, or personal aims, checklists are powerful machine that may be tailored. Individuals and organizations can also additionally growth their typical performance in their decided on fields of specialization with the aid of the usage of personalizing checklists to maximise their efficacy.

Industries and professions may additionally additionally have their very very very own set of responsibilities, techniques, and suggestions. Performance can be substantially superior and compliance may be assured via way of tailoring checklists to fit these unique desires. For instance, inside the hospitality quarter, checklists for hotel house obligations also can encompass duties like cleaning rooms, changing linens, and sanitizing lavatories, whilst checklists for the front table operations may moreover encompass obligations like guest take a look at-in, room challenge, and fee processing. Organizations can also make certain that each one required activities are executed efficiently and to the desired requirements through using developing enterprise-unique checklists.

There are pleasant regulations and norms for occupations including healthcare, constructing, and engineering. Professionals within the ones professions can also advantage from custom designed checklists through adhering to standard going for walks strategies, lowering mistakes, and ensuring compliance with industry suggestions. For example, inside the healthcare industry, checklists for the administration of medicinal capsules, affected person critiques, and contamination manage can also additionally assist healthcare professionals in adhering to extremely good practices and ensuring patient protection. Checklists for safety inspections, tool verifications, and nice manage may additionally useful resource inside the advent and engineering industries by manner of making sure that duties are completed in accordance with requirements and necessities.

Customized checklists may assist you obtain your personal goals. Checklists may additionally offer an prepared way to preserve song of chores and development, whether or not it's miles for handling non-public fee range, organizing a wedding, or attaining health goals. For instance, a fitness checklist can incorporate chores like workout plans, weight loss plan education, and development tracking, on the identical time as a marriage planning checklist might embody chores like venue desire, supplier coordination, and RSVPs. Individuals can also have greater achievement in attaining their very very very own desires by manner of the usage of using customized checklists to preserve organized, caused, and focused.

A checklist can be made mainly for a sure employer, career, or non-public purpose through using using customizing it to fulfill the ones needs and requirements. This can also moreover embody growing or condensing the listing of obligations, which includes high quality guidelines or pointers, and adjusting it to reflect the workflow or way for the vicinity of attention in question. With pertinent sports and instructions which might be appropriate to the specific scenario, customized checklists should be clean, succinct, and simple to apprehend.

To make sure that customized checklists continue to be successful, it is crucial to check and update them on a normal basis. Checklists should be up to date as essential to account for changing markets, occupations, and personal goals. The tick list may additionally additionally need to be improved a great way to better satisfy the desires and criteria, and enter from customers and stakeholders can be beneficial in figuring out these areas.

Chapter 12: Checklist Implementation Strategies

To clearly obtain the blessings of checklists, implementation issues from time to time stand up that ought to be resolved. The most not unusual barriers to tick list implementation are listed below, together with answers.

Resistance to Change

The biggest problem inside the usage of checklists is overcoming human beings's aversion to exchange. It's feasible that people are used to their gift strategies of doing subjects and may be reluctant to actually take delivery of a new device or device. It takes inexperienced trade control techniques to triumph over this problem. It's essential to supply the benefits of the usage of checklists, along with their expanded performance, decreased mistake price, and extra suitable results. Gaining the resource and possession of the crew with the useful resource of incorporating them in the advent and use of checklists is some different gain.

Lack of Standardization

Keeping uniformity for the duration of many groups or departments is some one-of-a-kind hassle. Checklists might also moreover range in shape, substance, or software program, ensuing in inconsistent efficacy. Setting up unique guidelines for growing and using checklists may additionally furthermore help assure uniformity and consistency. Giving businesses templates, instructions, and equipment to use as they devise standardized checklists may also be useful.

Limited Adoption and Compliance

It is probably difficult to ensure that checklists are extensively used and located. Checklists might not constantly be used by all group members, which reduces their usefulness. The merchandising of compliance may be assisted thru ongoing schooling, reminders, and overall performance evaluation. Greater adoption and compliance also can surrender result from putting in place a way of life that emphasizes and encourages the usage of checklists.

Lack of Flexibility

Checklists which may be overly strict and restrictive may not be suitable for all situations or processes. Adapting checklists to a collection's specific requirements or situation can be difficult. It's vital to create checklists which may be adaptive and versatile, allowing for adjustment in step with the scenario or environment. Checklists can be stored contemporary-day and beneficial at some stage in time through the use of being reviewed and up to date on a regular foundation.

Integration into Workflow

It is probably difficult to integrate checklists into modern-day strategies. Teams may not surely encompass checklists if they're visible as a similarly responsibility or burden.

Checklists may be covered greater without problems into everyday workflows by being brought to contemporary structures, gear, or techniques. Checklists' usability and integration into modern tactics may additionally additionally each be improved via automating them using digital systems or software program.

Sustaining Momentum

Maintaining momentum in the use of checklists is probably difficult after the number one installation. Checklists may moreover in the end lose their usefulness if they'll be not constantly bolstered. The use of checklists may also hold to advantage traction with ordinary tracking, remarks, and basic overall performance reviews. Checklists can be made more treasured and crucial via recognizing and applauding accomplishments made viable via manner of the use of them.

Overall, placing checklists into workout successfully can be tough, but the ones troubles can be solved with foresight.

Overcoming opposition to exchange, assuring consistency, encouraging adoption and compliance, imparting flexibility, incorporating checklists into strategies, and keeping momentum are critical issues that need hobby. By overcoming the ones obstacles, groups may additionally additionally furthermore genuinely understand checklists' functionality as powerful device for raising productivity, strengthening choice-making, and streamlining procedures. Checklists may be efficaciously covered and utilized in an entire lot of fields, occupations, and private pursuits with suitable schooling, communique, and persevering with tracking.

Strategies For Integrating Checklists Into Existing Workflows And Processes

In many unique professions and sectors, checklists are powerful device that might growth output, accuracy, and performance. It can be hard to include checklists into modern-day workflows and techniques, but, because it calls for cautious training, coordination, and exchange manage. The following strategies let you integrate checklists efficaciously into cutting-edge workflows and methods.

Understand Current Workflows

It is essential to have a complete statistics of the winning workflows and methods earlier than introducing checklists. This includes identifying the workflow's many techniques, obligations, and responsibilities and punctiliously documenting them. You may additionally additionally find places in which checklists might be beneficial and the method streamlined through developing a radical preserve close of the contemporary workflow.

Identify High-Impact Areas

It's important to pinpoint excessive-effect areas wherein checklists also can drastically beautify workflow after you have got an intensive preserve close to of the current manner. These might be important strategies or levels that are vulnerable to mistakes or omissions, or places wherein standardization and uniformity are essential. You may also moreover deliver tick list integration pinnacle precedence and assure gold favored fulfillment by means of using identifying the ones immoderate-impact regions.

Collaborate with Stakeholders

Collaboration with key stakeholders engaged inside the method is important for the a fulfillment integration of checklists. Members of the team, control, and distinct pertinent occasions can be included here. To consistent their assist and ownership of the approach, embody stakeholders within the components and execution of checklists. Encourage stakeholder enter and pointers in order that checklists may be tailor-made to their unique requirements and options.

Develop Customized Checklists

Incorporating checklists into present day strategies efficiently calls for personalization. Create checklists which might be precise to the obligations, roles, and duties which can be part of the system. When developing checklists, maintain in thoughts the precise limits and goals of the workflow. Doing so will assist the checklists glide glaringly with the current method. To sell common use, make checklists succinct, clean, and aesthetically attractive.

Provide Adequate Training and Resources

To permit the effective integration of checklists, exact sufficient training and belongings are important. Train organization contributors successfully on how to utilize the checklists and put in force them into their regular exercises. Provide equipment to help the proper use of checklists, together with templates, instructions, and venture aids. Ensure that the checklists are available to group individuals and that they may be privy to their significance to the machine.

Monitor and Review Usage

To preserve efficacy, tick list utilization need to be regularly reviewed and monitored. Checklist use is monitored, institution people' opinions are accrued, and their outcomes on workflow are evaluated. Checklists must be reviewed and up to date on a everyday basis to make certain they will be regardless of the fact that beneficial and powerful. Optimize the checklists for the splendid outcomes through using overall performance records and comments to pinpoint areas that want paintings.

Foster a Culture of Checklist Usage

For integration to be effective, it is vital to cultivate a lifestyle that values and encourages the use of checklists. Team humans that use checklists often ought to be praised and recognized for their achievements. Encourage the improvement of a way of life of continuous improvement wherein the usage of checklists is valued, acknowledged, and guarded into crew sports activities on a everyday basis.

In summary, incorporating checklists into contemporary workflows and strategies requires cautious planning, coordination, and alternate management. Successful integration calls for some of important techniques, such as an statistics of the winning workflows, the identification of excessive-impact regions, collaboration with stakeholders, the development of tailored checklists, provision of suitable education and assets, tracking and evaluation of use, and the vending of a subculture of checklist utilization. Following the ones hints can help businesses put into effect checklists into workflows and strategies with out problem, resulting in improved productiveness, accuracy, and performance at some point of pretty a number of sectors and professions.

Training And Onboarding For Checklist Adoption

The effectiveness of checklists is predicated closely on proper education and onboarding of group individuals who is probably the usage of them. Below are the significance of training and onboarding for successful tick list adoption and the way businesses can make certain that their groups are nicely-equipped to utilize checklists to their fullest capability.

Understanding the Purpose and Benefits of Checklists

Starting with a easy maintain near of the function and benefits of checklists is essential for education and onboarding. The importance of checklists, how they might streamline workflow, and the manner they will have an effect on group contributors' accuracy and productivity have to all be understood through all members. This should be introduced in a way that emphasizes the importance of checklists and the way they relate to their specific responsibilities and duties.

Providing Comprehensive Instruction on Checklist Usage

A thorough explanation of the manner to utilize checklists should be included in proper education. This includes describing the format of checklists, the way to use them, a manner to read and understand them, how to test off gadgets as they're completed, and the manner to replace and alter them as vital. For crew members to feel at ease and confident using checklists of their each day art work, it's far critical to provide them real-global examples and possibilities for workout.

Customizing Checklists for Specific Roles and Tasks

It's possible for one among a kind institution individuals to have numerous roles, obligations, and obligations that name for using checklists. Checklists want to be especially tailor-made to the roles and responsibilities of every company member. To try this, it can be important to designate particular checklists for severa departments, groups, or obligations and to alter the shape and content material of the checklists as crucial. The use of customization makes certain that group members can rapid hook up with and use the checklists in their very personal work environments.

Providing Ongoing Support and Resources

Onboarding and training need to be non-stop procedures in preference to a one-time event. To ensure that company human beings have get right of entry to to the device and records they want to make use of checklists efficiently, organizations need to provide non-stop help and sources. This need to encompass offering checklist templates, commands, venture aids, and different materials that group participants can use as a reference. Refresher schooling, feedback durations, and everyday test-ins may additionally moreover furthermore all assist organization contributors revel in more strongly approximately the rate of checklists and address any troubles they'll be having.

Incorporating Checklists into Onboarding for New Hires

Checklists must be introduced to new personnel at some degree in the onboarding approach to assure early uptake. Checklists need to be a part of the onboarding process for trendy personnel so they may be privy to a manner to use them and their advantages from the begin. By ensuring that new institution individuals have the talents wanted to make use of checklists successfully of their jobs, this can help installation a subculture of checklist use in the organization.

Encouraging Feedback and Continuous Improvement

When enhancing checklists for max effectiveness, group member feedback is essential. Encourage crew individuals to percentage their insights, provide pointers for upgrades, and offer remarks on how checklists are being used. This enter can be used to pinpoint troubles or potential regions for improvement and permit ongoing checklist enhancement to hold them beneficial and green in some unspecified time within the future of the manner.

Leading by the use of Example

The use of checklists internal an corporation is strongly encouraged thru manage. Leaders can set a superb instance thru frequently the use of checklists of their personal each day workout routines. Leaders can also furthermore encourage organization people to conform with their lead and take delivery of using checklists as a ordinary approach in the place of work via offering an notable example.

Ultimately, powerful tick list adoption interior a enterprise employer relies upon on good enough education and onboarding. Key techniques for incorporating checklists into contemporary workflows and techniques embody information the motive and advantages of checklists, giving thorough instructions, customizing checklists for specific roles and duties, providing ongoing help and assets, collectively with checklists in new hire onboarding, encouraging feedback and non-save you development, and setting an splendid instance. The danger that group humans may also see checklists as a beneficial device for reinforcing their productivity, accuracy, and efficiency at work will increase with right training and onboarding.

Chapter 13: Checklist For Daily Life

Many people war with the various, pressing final dates, duties, and responsibilities in current day speedy-paced society. Being prepared and maintaining song of everything may be tough, which could increase strain and decrease productivity. Checklists may additionally additionally keep the day in this case. Checklists are clean however powerful tools that can be used for numerous private desires, along with productiveness, business business enterprise, and self-development.

The crucial use of checklists in each day lifestyles is to boom productiveness. An organized tick list may also additionally moreover function as a street map, directing people thru their duties and helping in their choice-making about priority. Individuals also can make sure that now not anything slips thru the cracks and that they keep attention on their dreams through manner of developing a checklist of chores to be completed in a day, week, or month. A feeling of fulfillment and idea to go to the subsequent hobby are supplied via crossing off subjects at the list as they will be completed.

Additionally useful for growing organizational abilities are checklists. It might be difficult to bear in thoughts all your duties, appointments, and duties. People may also installation the way they hold track in their sports sports and responsibilities by means of way of manner of creating checklists for loads components of their lives, together with paintings, domestic, and private. A checklist for art work may also encompass due dates and important conferences, on the equal time as one for home could consist of errands to be completed, bills to be paid, and appointments to be made. Creating checklists for chores also can help humans hold prepared, live on pinnacle of their obligations, and feel an entire lot less pressured.

Another area wherein checklists can be correctly used is in the place of self-development. Checklists can be used as a tool for measuring development and keeping motivation, whether or now not or not it is getting to know a new capability, adopting a healthy way of existence, or pursuing personal targets. For example, a checklist for learning a ultra-modern expertise can comprise high excellent moves to be finished, tool to make use of, and goals to obtain. People also can keep on the proper song, gauge their improvement, and recognize their accomplishments with the aid of manner of periodically reviewing and updating the checklist.

Checklists can be used for some of one-of-a-type private dreams, which embody experience training, occasion planning, and ordinary exercises, similarly to productivity, business business enterprise, and self-development. For example, a tick list for making plans a adventure can also moreover comprise things like packing the requirements, reserving adventure and hotels, and arranging for transportation, at the same time as a tick list for organizing an event would possibly possibly consist of such things as traveller lists, meal making plans, and decorations. Checklists also can be used to simplify day by day workout routines which incorporates morning and night time sporting activities, exercise routines, and meals education.

Each man or woman's particular sports, desires, and priorities ought to be cautiously taken into consideration at the same time as developing checklists for personal use. Here are some tips for growing inexperienced checklists:

Keep it smooth: The reason of a tick list is to simplify responsibilities, so keep the tick list itself easy and clean to apprehend. Use clean and concise language, and avoid useless complexity.

Be precise: Include particular responsibilities, remaining dates, and milestones in the checklist to provide a smooth roadmap for final touch. This permits to avoid ambiguity and ensures that responsibilities are completed in a properly timed manner.

Prioritize: Organize responsibilities so as of priority, in order that the most important and time-sensitive responsibilities are at the top of the listing. This permits human beings live targeted on what desires to be completed first.

Review and update regularly: Review the checklist regularly to make certain that it remains updated and relevant. Update it as desired based totally mostly on changing priorities or improvement made.

Celebrate achievements: Checking off devices on the tick list can offer a feel of achievement. Celebrate small victories and milestones to stay inspired and endorsed.

As a quit give up result, checklists are effective gear that can be carried out in each day existence to growth productivity, employer, and self-development. Individuals might also live focused, organized, and recommended on the identical time as running via their sports and attaining their goals with the resource of using well-installed checklists. For maximum effectiveness, checklists must be periodically reviewed and updated. Checklists can be tailored to positive factors of your lifestyles, which incorporates hobby, domestic, excursion, occasions, and normal sports. Individuals can also additionally simplify their jobs, conquer obstacles, and decorate their productivity and organizational abilties with the useful resource of incorporating checklists into their personal workflows and techniques. Checklists may be an effective tool for reaching personal fulfillment and improvement with the precise thoughts-set and method. So why no longer try it and find out how checklists may additionally additionally alternate your non-public productiveness, employer, and direction to self-improvement? Create your private checklists proper now and discover the tremendous results they will have to your each day lifestyles.

Checklists For Household Chores, Travel, Financial Management, And Other Aspects Of Daily Life

In addition to being useful in expert contexts, checklists may be quite useful in lots of excellent additives of ordinary existence. Checklists may additionally aid humans in being organized, powerful, and targeted whilst completing sports activities which includes domestic chores, tour preparations, and coins control. In this publish, we will study how checklists can be used out of doors of the workplace and one-of-a-kind formal contexts in lots of factors of everyday life.

Checklists are pretty beneficial for quite some duties, along with home responsibilities. Cleaning, organizing, doing laundry, food purchasing, and awesome each day duties are all essential to maintain a residence tidy and properly-maintained. Making a tick list of those duties can also moreover help humans remain on top of their home responsibilities and make certain that not something is disregarded. Every own family's precise desires may be met by means of manner of the usage of tailoring a tick list, which can be organized primarily based totally totally on each day, weekly, monthly, or seasonal duties. People can also prevent vain worry, keep time and energy, and maintain their homes easy and prepared through the use of a easy checklist as a guide.

Checklists may be pretty useful even as organizing a adventure, it's far every other place. No depend the length of the journey—whether it's miles a short weekend damage or a prolonged worldwide adventure—making plans entails hundreds of factors, which embody scheduling flights, resorts, transportation, packing, journey papers, and activities. A excursion training checklist can preserve humans prepared, guarantee that no longer some thing is forgotten, and make the enjoy easy and first-class. Among the matters on a journey tick list are passports, visas, tickets, a packing listing, an itinerary, excursion insurance, and further. A thorough journey checklist might also moreover assist people make certain they have the whole lot they need for his or her journey and save you ultimate-minute complications.

An crucial a part of ordinary living that checklists may additionally moreover help with substantially is economic control. It can be tough to preserve track of fees, charge range, pay bills, and manage property, in particular whilst there are many unique financial duties to take care of. Making a tick list for financial control can also help humans continue to be prepared, make sure that their bills are paid on time, hold tune in their spending, and manipulate their coins nicely. Monthly expenses, financial financial savings goals, investment monitoring, credit card payments, and various factors might also additionally all be blanketed on a tick list for economic manage. Individuals also can take fee in their very very own cash by using way of the usage of a tick list to get a clean photo in their monetary duties.

Checklists can be used for numerous ordinary responsibilities, which include home chores, organizing journeys, and cash management. Checklists may be used, amongst special matters, to time table meals, exercising exercises, self-care wearing activities, domestic improvement duties, and sports. People also can control their non-public lives more successfully and effectively by manner of way of growing checklists which might be tailor-made to high-quality factors of normal life an first rate manner to remain organized, powerful, and targeted.

Chapter 14: Troubleshooting And Optimizing Checklists

Checklists are powerful device which can extensively enhance productivity, judgment, and industrial organisation company. They do have high quality guidelines and dangers, however, similar to any tool.

One everyday mistake while the usage of checklists is to end up excessively dependent on them and regard them as rigid jail recommendations. Although checklists are supposed to offer an organized framework for finishing sports, they need to not be visible as strict directives that have to be adhered to without question. The purpose of a tick list is to serve as a reference, but it need to additionally be flexible and adaptable relying at the perfect situation. As humans may additionally moreover actually tick topics off the listing with out thinking about the complexities of the situation, an overreliance on checklists can also bring about a loss of essential questioning, creativity, and trouble-fixing talents. To keep away from falling into this trap, it is essential to apply checklists as a tool to decorate choice-making in preference to as a inflexible set of pointers and to promote flexibility and vital thinking at the same time as using them.

Failure to robotically update checklists is some different fault people make at the equal time as using them. The purpose of a tick list is not to create a static document that in no manner modifications. Checklists have to be stored updated on the way to be effective whilst you take into account that duties, procedures, and necessities could probably change through the years. Updated records, obligations which can be unnoticed, and possible errors can also additionally all give up end result from failing to replace checklists. To preserve checklists present day-day and accurate, the method want to consist of ordinary assessment and updating of the files.

A 1/3 mistake people make whilst using checklists isn't always tailoring them to first rate situations or sports. Generic checklists are beneficial, but they will no longer commonly cover the special needs and wishes of a certain difficulty, career, or system. One-duration-suits-all techniques may additionally moreover provide checklists that aren't in reality optimized for the unique environment, ensuing in inefficiencies and errors. It's crucial to tailor checklists to the appropriate region, career, or interest reachable and to do not forget elements like guidelines, corporation first-rate practices, and specific requirements while growing or the use of checklists.

Neglecting the human element is each different mistake made while the usage of checklists. Although they may be tools created to guide human widespread general overall performance, checklists cannot take the place of human discretion and information. It may result in mistakes and oversights to depend best on checklists without taking into consideration human additives like intuition, experience, and communique skills. It's important to utilize checklists in addition to human judgment in choice to rather for it. The usage of checklists can be made greater inexperienced thru using encouraging open conversation, a subculture of continual improvement, and the development of vital thinking skills.

The failure to include stakeholders inside the development and use of checklists can also be a ordinary mistake. To make sure that checklists are thorough, accurate, and beneficial, stakeholders like group participants, personnel, or relevant experts may offer insightful remarks. Stakeholder participation also can inspire ownership, duty, and self-control to the tick list, so that you can decorate its adoption and execution.

Ultimately, checklists can be effective equipment for developing typical overall performance and business enterprise enterprise, however they may be not errors-free. When the use of checklists, frequent mistakes encompass relying an excessive amount of on them, failing to replace them, failing to customise them, ignoring the human detail, and failing to embody stakeholders. To maximize the blessings of checklists, workflows and techniques can be nicely included with them by means of way of being privy to the ones possible dangers and taking the crucial movements to triumph over them. When used nicely, checklists may be very beneficial gear for developing output, decreasing mistakes, and getting higher consequences in a number of contexts.

Strategies For Troubleshooting And Optimizing Checklists For Continuous Improvement

Using checklists can also moreover moreover appreciably growth performance and accuracy for the cause that they offer a scientific framework for system of entirety. To assure their efficacy over time, checklists can also, like numerous device, have issues or want to be optimized. The techniques for troubleshooting and enhancing checklists for non-prevent development are indexed below.

Regular Review and Feedback Loops

Establishing a way for ordinary assessment and remarks loops is one efficient method for enhancing checklists. To spot any viable issues or opportunities for development, checklists should be routinely reviewed. This can be finished via way of mission a self-assessment or via soliciting input from stakeholders, which include organization members or relevant specialists. The checklist may additionally want to be up to date due to remarks that may help identify any inaccuracies, gaps, or out-of-date data. Setting up a remarks loop lets in the tick list to be advanced continuously, ensuring that it remains applicable and useful inside the ever-changing surroundings.

Performance Metrics and Data Analysis

Establishing prevalent normal overall performance measurements and doing statistics evaluation is every other method for reinforcing checklists. Insights on the usefulness of the checklist may be derived by using manner of gathering and comparing facts on its normal typical performance, which includes very last touch charges, accuracy, and outcomes. Data evaluation can be used to discover patterns, dispositions, or places in which checklist utilization is probably stepped forward. To resolve issues placed and improve the tick list's basic performance, this information can be used to replace or adjust it.

User Feedback and Input

Participating tick list clients within the development method can be really beneficial. Users are within the system of placing the tick list into movement and might offer insightful critiques on its benefits, dangers, and viable regions for development. Surveys, interviews, or awareness agencies may be used to get individual comments and enter, and this qualitative records can be used to update or regulate the checklist. In order to decorate elegance and execution of the checklist, consumer enter may additionally additionally create possession and buy-in.

Continuous Training and Development

Giving checklist customers ongoing schooling and growth possibilities is a vital factor of a few exclusive crucial method for tick list optimization. Users may be educated to comprehend the tick list's dreams, blessings, and accurate use. It may additionally provide clients the risk to alternate super practices, studies from each other, and address any issues or queries they may have with the checklist. Users may also moreover furthermore improve their expertise and skills via ongoing schooling, if you need to permit them to make use of the checklist more successfully and successfully.

Customization and Adaptation

To the best scenario or artwork at hand, checklists need to be often modified and changed. The checklist need to be revised to account for adjustments even as sports, techniques, or requirements evolve. Incorporating consumer comments and input, in addition to enhancing the tick list to meet the requirements of other sectors, professions, or jobs, all fall under the elegance of customization. The checklist is automatically changed and custom designed to assure its endured applicability, accuracy, and efficacy inside the precise state of affairs, which promotes top common performance.

Technology and Automation

Another tactic for checklist optimization is to make use of generation and automation. Technology answers, such assignment management software program program, assignment control software program application software, or checklist packages, also can automate repetitive chores, improve the checklist device, and provide real-time comments or reminders. Automation also can boom the tick list's regular efficacy by way of the usage of the use of reducing mistakes, developing productiveness, and developing standard performance. Over-reliance on technology, even though, can also bring about complacency or mistakes, so it's far vital to create a balance among it and human judgment.

Collaboration and Communication

Collaboration and conversation amongst group human beings or checklist customers also can be a a achievement technique for checklist optimization and troubleshooting. Promoting cooperation among customers, building a culture of non-stop development, and encouraging open communique may also additionally moreover offer insightful thoughts, proposals, and answers for improving the checklist. The organization may fit collectively to perceive and join any faults or holes within the checklist with the aid of using sharing its contributors' studies, problems, and extraordinary practices. The imaginitive thoughts, expanded recognition, and greater suitable regular effectiveness of the tick list can also additionally all end end result from this collaborative approach.

Continuous Monitoring and Evaluation

For optimization, it's miles crucial to continuously display and confirm the checklist's standard average performance. It is viable to get insights into regions that want development via monitoring the tick list's overall performance on a ordinary foundation, quantifying its efficacy, and assessing its effect on productivity, accuracy, and effects. Quantitative measurements like final touch expenses, mistake fees, or time taken, as well as qualitative ones like person comments, stakeholder input, or commentary, may be used for monitoring and assessment. To ensure the checklist stays beneficial, updates, tweaks, or optimizations can be made based absolutely at the findings of the monitoring and assessment.

Flexibility and Adaptability

It's vital to understand that checklists are dynamic gadget in preference to static records, and that they want to be fluid and adaptive. The checklist must be flexible enough to adjust whilst obligations or requirements do. Long-time period relevancy and effectiveness of the checklist can be ensured thru being open to alternate, prepared to alter or update the checklist in response to remarks or new facts, and flexible in its use.

Leadership and Accountability

The closing hassle in checklist optimization is manage and responsibility. Leaders need to promote the fee of the usage of checklists, make certain that the checklist is covered into the manner, and assist a non-save you development manner of existence. The checklist need for use successfully, and group individuals need to be held answerable for this. Leaders need to moreover help troubleshooting and optimization efforts by using the usage of the usage of imparting assets and assist. Leaders also can make certain the tick list is used correctly and optimized for max effect via the use of manner of building an surroundings of responsibility.

Chapter 15: Measuring The Impact Of Checklists

To ensure that checklists are quality their meant characteristic and generating the expected outcomes, it is important to evaluate their efficacy. In quite a few industries, at the facet of healthcare, aviation, banking, challenge management, and ordinary dwelling, checklists are beneficial tool that may increase productivity, accuracy, and desire-making. However, without a doubt setting up checklists with out assessing their efficacy can also result in the lack of probabilities for optimization and improvement.

Setting Clear goals

Setting smooth dreams is the primary degree in assessing the efficacy of checklists. What goals does utilizing the checklist preference to gain? What goals are you attempting to satisfy? Setting benchmarks and standards for comparing the efficacy of the tick list is made possible via manner of in fact defining your dreams. A checklist's efficacy, as an example, can be assessed through the years primarily based mostly on what number of treatment mistakes have decreased if its aim is to prevent medicine errors in a healthcare context.

Data Collection

Both quantitative and qualitative facts need to be amassed if you want to test the fulfillment of checklists. Measurable metrics, such of entirety fees, mistake prices, time required, or first-rate average overall performance signs and symptoms, are part of quantitative statistics. Subjective comments, client enter, stakeholder perspectives, or unique qualitative measurements of the tick list's impact are all examples of qualitative facts. The series of every styles of records lets in a more thorough assessment and offers a whole image of the efficacy of the tick list.

Using Performance Metrics

Performance metrics are essential for assessing how well checklists work. You may additionally decide the checklist's have an impact on on a range of things, which incorporates productivity, accuracy, overall performance, and consequences, via placing performance measures referring to the goals of the tick list. The average performance degree can be the percentage growth in finished obligations after the adoption of the checklist, as an example, if a checklist is finished in a venture control state of affairs to raise mission of entirety expenses. Performance metrics provide quantifiable facts that may be reviewed and measured in opposition to predetermined necessities to see if the checklist is strolling as supposed.

Data evaluation

Data assessment is essential in case you want to discover dispositions, styles, and insights once statistics has been gathered. Data assessment can also help in discovering possible troubles, locating trouble regions, and locating optimization possibilities. It's important to bear in mind qualitative enter from clients, stakeholders, or one of a kind pertinent activities further to quantitative facts. Qualitative remarks may also furthermore offer insightful statistics at the usability, usefulness, and effect of the tick list on the entire procedure. Analyzing each quantitative and qualitative facts will let you get an entire information of the fulfillment of the tick list.

Comparing Against Benchmarks and desires

In order to assess the efficacy of checklists, it's miles crucial to evaluate the facts amassed with diagnosed benchmarks and goals. Benchmarks are preset benchmarks which might be established using first-class practices, ancient facts, or enterprise norms. The desired effects that have been unique while the tick list emerge as positioned into use are referred to as the goals. You may moreover moreover take a look at if the tick list is undertaking its dreams or falling brief in superb respects with the useful resource of evaluating the amassed facts to these benchmarks and desires. You can pinpoint areas that need improvement or optimization using this assessment.

Obtaining User and Stakeholder enter

An important step in assessing the efficacy of checklists is to get individual and stakeholder input. The checklist's actual customers also can provide insightful feedback on its usefulness, usability, and impact on their workflow. Stakeholders can also moreover provide insight into how the tick list aligns with enterprise dreams, compliance wishes, and distinct strategic objectives. Stakeholders can encompass managers, supervisors, or special pertinent events. Users' and stakeholders' comments may also thing out feasible issues, provide improvements, and thing out regions that want to be stepped forward.

Examining Contextual elements

Contextual elements that would have an effect on the overall common overall performance of checklists want to be taken into consideration at the identical time as evaluating their efficacy. Contextual variables may also moreover encompass matters just like the specific installing which the tick list is being used, the trouble of the responsibilities being finished, the clients' talent degrees, and different things. Due to the only of a type sports, techniques, and requirements, a tick list that works well in a clinic context might not paintings as well in a economic one. Contextual issues offer a extra nuanced evaluation of the tick list's fulfillment and useful resource in figuring out areas that might need change or exchange.

Integrating Continuous Improvement

Assessing the performance of checklists is a non-prevent interest in desire to a one-time event. It's vital to have a non-forestall improvement manner of life wherein remarks, records, and insights are continuously done to decorate the tick list. This includes robotically evaluating the effectiveness of the checklist, locating regions for improvement, and putting updates or revisions into movement as critical. The tick list is stored modern, useful, and consistent with the converting requirements of the customers and the enterprise via non-stop development.

Sharing Results and Acting

Sharing Results and Acting need to be included in the assessment of the efficacy of checklists, further to information evaluation and comments accumulating. To increase recognition, inspire obligation, and beneficial useful aid in desire-making, it's far important to share the assessment findings with the best stakeholders, which include clients, managers, and great preference-makers. Action want to be made to rectify any faults placed, placed updates or revisions into area, and continuously growth the efficacy of the tick list primarily based absolutely at the assessment findings.

Flexibility and Adaptability

Finally, it is important to apprehend that checklists also can need to be flexible and adaptive if you want to address converting situations. To guarantee persevering with effectiveness, the tick list can also additionally want to be changed or up to date if workflows, methods, or requirements exchange. It is critical to don't forget that assessing the efficacy of checklists is a dynamic, persevering with way that takes into account the customers' changing desires similarly to the context wherein they're being applied.

In order to ensure that checklists are alluring their intended motive and producing the expected effects, it's miles essential to evaluate their efficacy. The effectiveness of checklists may be assessed the use of strategies like setting clean desires, gathering quantitative and qualitative statistics, the use of ordinary normal performance metrics, studying statistics and comments, evaluating in opposition to benchmarks and objectives, getting character and stakeholder feedback, incorporating non-save you improvement, speaking consequences, and incorporating flexibility and adaptableness. Organizations can make sure they may be the usage of the complete ability of these formidable gear to enhance productivity, accuracy, and desire-making in quite some regions and spheres of life thru often reading and improving checklists.

Methods For Measuring The Impact Of Checklists On Productivity, Accuracy, And Outcomes

Individuals and companies can also use checklists to quick and effectively accomplish their objectives. But how can the effectiveness of checklists be measured?

Quantitative Metrics

Utilizing quantitative metrics is an everyday way to assess the effectiveness of checklists. These are quantifiable, intention facts elements that could provide quantitative proof of the fulfillment of the tick list. Quantitative measures in the healthcare enterprise, as an example, might be the decline in pharmaceutical errors, the drop in clinic-obtained infections, or the enhancement of affected man or woman effects. Quantitative metrics within the context of undertaking management would possibly possibly consist of the decline in venture delays, the upward push in on-time transport, or the enhancement in mission notable. Organizations might also moreover evaluate the quantifiable outcomes of checklists on output, accuracy, and productivity with the aid of using monitoring and comparing those quantitative measures.

Qualitative Feedback

Receiving qualitative comments is a few other manner to evaluate the effectiveness of checklists. This includes gathering arbitrary input regarding users' perceptions of the tick list from stakeholders, stakeholders, and different relevant parties. Qualitative comments may additionally offer insightful information at the efficacy, usability, and impact of the checklist on workflow and preference-making. For instance, getting qualitative comments from physicians and nurses on how the checklist has stepped forward their workflow, decreased cognitive load, or extended verbal exchange and collaboration might be done in a hospital putting. Obtaining qualitative remarks inside the context of private productivity need to encompass asking human beings how the tick list has helped them in maintaining employer, prioritizing their chores, or reaching their desires. Using qualitative feedback, organizations can also research greater about the human factor in tick list execution, which enhances quantitative measurements.

Benchmarking

Benchmarking is a specific way to evaluate the effectiveness of checklists. Benchmarking consists of evaluating a manner' or undertaking's fashionable common overall performance with familiar norms or recommended practices. Organizations also can examine the boom in productivity, accuracy, and outcomes via benchmarking the performance of sports activities or techniques before and after tick list adoption. For instance, benchmarking in the finance industry can embody contrasting the timeliness and correctness of economic reporting earlier than and after the adoption of a checklist for monetary reconciliation. Benchmarking within the context of home chores may also additionally consist of contrasting the period of time had to do sports with and without the beneficial resource of a checklist. Organizations also can examine the general overall performance of checklists in accomplishing supposed consequences through benchmarking, which offers a evaluation view.

Studies through declaration

Studies thru observation are another way to evaluate the effectiveness of checklists. Observational research entail monitoring qualitative or quantitative facts on how human beings or companies whole sports or strategies each with and with out the use of a tick list. For example, observational research in a hospital context can also entail recording records on the adherence to protocols, accuracy of documentation, and affected character consequences on the equal time as tracking physicians and nurses as they conduct patient rounds each with and with out using a checklist. In a mission manipulate setting, observational studies should encompass tracking records on project shipping, remarkable, and progress as challenge groups perform obligations each with and with out the usage of a tick list. Observational research offer sensible knowledge on how checklists have an effect on actual performance and outcomes.

User surveys

User surveys are some other manner to evaluate the effectiveness of checklists. Users who've used a tick list are surveyed to find out about their perspectives, critiques, and results. User surveys can be created to accumulate facts on loads of implementation-related subjects, collectively with person happiness, usability, productivity impact, accuracy, and effects. As they record subjective enter on how the checklist has affected their average overall performance and effects, individual surveys may additionally acquire crucial statistics about the efficacy of checklists from the client's factor of view. For instance, acquiring comments from tourists on how a excursion checklist has helped them live organized, decrease pressure, and make sure they have got everything they need for their journey is one manner to make use of man or woman surveys in a journey context. User surveys may additionally furthermore provide insightful feedback on how checklists are looked as though it would work and component up regions that could need alternate or customisation.

Post-Implementation opinions

Another manner to assess the effectiveness of checklists is to conduct located up-implementation critiques. In submit-implementation critiques, the efficacy of the checklist is classed after it is been achieved in real situations. To determine the have an effect on of the tick list on output, accuracy, and productivity, opinions, audits, or evaluations can be accomplished. For instance, a post-implementation evaluation inside the banking agency might embody assessing the timeliness and amazing of monetary opinions produced the use of a checklist. In the context of domestic chores, a put up-implementation assessment would possibly likely encompass comparing the efficacy and overall performance of chores completed the use of a tick list. Post-implementation critiques provide a look over again at the effect of the tick list and can useful useful resource groups in figuring out areas for improvement and improvement.

Iterative Feedback and Improvement

Last however not least, a persistent feedback loop and improvement tool may be used to evaluate the effectiveness of checklists. This involves collecting person, stakeholder, and extremely good pertinent occasions' enter on a everyday foundation and using it to modify and decorate the tick list. Organizations also can continuously have a have a look at and improve the efficacy of the checklist over the years the usage of this iterative technique. For example, in a task management placing, challenge companies might also provide input at the usability, applicability, and affect of the tick list on consequences, which may be used to replace and enhance it. The tick list is saved up to date with the sports or strategies it is supposed to help further to the customers' evolving desires manner to this constant remarks and improvement system.

Overall, masses of strategies, along with quantitative metrics, qualitative feedback, benchmarking, observational studies, character surveys, publish-implementation evaluations, and iterative feedback and improvement techniques, may be used to assess the consequences of checklists on productiveness, accuracy, and consequences. Combining those techniques may moreover offer an intensive perception of the tick list's efficacy and capability improvement regions. Organizations can also usually enhance the use of checklists, assure their efficacy, and gain their goals efficiently and efficaciously with the useful resource of assessing the effect of checklists.

Chapter 16: Real World Examples Of Checklist Success

Checklists have confirmed to be effective system for boosting productiveness, improving accuracy, and optimizing effects throughout severa fields and industries. Real-global case research offer compelling proof of the a fulfillment implementation of checklists in severa settings. Let's delve into some noteworthy examples of a achievement checklist implementation and discover the advantages and training located out from those case studies.

Healthcare: The World Health Organization (WHO) Surgical Safety Checklist

The WHO Surgical Safety Checklist is a globally recognized example of tick list implementation in healthcare settings. Developed with the aid of the usage of a team of specialists, this checklist pastimes to decorate affected individual protection at some point of surgical procedures with the useful resource of standardizing crucial protection checks before, inside the course of, and after surgical strategies. Studies have tested that the use of the WHO Surgical Safety Checklist has caused a large reduce rate in surgical complications and mortality prices in numerous healthcare centers international.

The success of the WHO Surgical Safety Checklist may be attributed to numerous factors, which consist of its simplicity, comprehensive insurance of crucial protection assessments, and the collaborative nature of its implementation. The checklist is designed to be utilized by the whole surgical group, fostering effective communique and teamwork, and promoting a culture of protection. The tick list has been included into the workflow of surgical groups and has emerge as a contemporary exercising in plenty of healthcare centers, contributing to improved affected individual consequences.

Aviation: The Boeing 737 MAX Checklist Update

In the aviation organisation, checklists are critical for ensuring the safety and normal performance of flights. The case of the Boeing 737 MAX aircraft gives an exciting instance of the way checklist implementation can play a pivotal function in addressing annoying situations and enhancing outcomes. Following the tragic injuries regarding the Boeing 737 MAX plane in 2018 and 2019, Boeing recognized troubles with the aircraft's tick list and completed updates to deal with the deficiencies.

The tick list updates included clearer instructions for dealing with the plane's Maneuvering Characteristics Augmentation System (MCAS), which have emerge as diagnosed as a contributing trouble in the injuries. The updates moreover integrated remarks from pilots and regulators to beautify the usability and effectiveness of the tick list. The revised tick list was implemented as a part of the aircraft's revised running techniques and has been instrumental in restoring take shipping of as genuine with inside the protection and reliability of the Boeing 737 MAX plane.

Finance: Investment Decision-Making Checklist

Checklists also are precious equipment inside the finance business enterprise, in which accuracy and hobby to detail are essential for making sound funding alternatives. Hedge fund supervisor and writer, Mohnish Pabrai, stocks a awesome case study in his ebook "The Dhandho Investor," wherein he achieved a whole funding preference-making tick list primarily based totally on the concepts of cost making an investment.

Pabrai's checklist consists of a chain of questions and criteria that he makes use of to assess funding possibilities. By strictly adhering to the tick list, Pabrai has been capable of make informed funding picks with a disciplined and systematic method. His checklist has helped him keep away from steeply-priced errors and acquire ordinary funding returns, making it a a hit example of checklist implementation within the finance corporation.

Project Management: Construction Project Checklist

In the sector of challenge control, checklists can play a essential feature in making sure the a fulfillment crowning glory of complex tasks. One example is the implementation of a advent assignment checklist thru a huge introduction company. The tick list consists of diverse obligations, which include acquiring lets in, carrying out protection inspections, and coordinating with subcontractors, which need to be finished at exceptional degrees of the improvement system.

The implementation of the development mission checklist has delivered about superior task coordination, streamlined conversation, and decreased remodel, leading to greater green project delivery and increased consumer pride. The checklist serves as a entire guide for project managers and employer individuals, ensuring that critical responsibilities aren't disregarded and venture timelines are adhered to.

Lessons Learned

These real-worldwide case studies of a hit checklist implementation spotlight numerous key education:

Simplicity and comprehensiveness: Successful checklists have to be simple and easy to recognize, on the equal time as moreover shielding all vital responsibilities and exams to ensure accuracy and productivity.

Collaborative implementation: Checklists are high-quality even as they're used collaboratively by way of the entire team or frame of humans, fostering effective communique, coordination, and teamwork.

Continuous development: Checklists want to be frequently reviewed and updated based totally on feedback from clients, lessons found out from errors, and changes in the industry or environment. Continuous development ensures that the checklists live relevant and effective through the years.

Integration into workflows and techniques: Checklists must be incorporated seamlessly into present workflows and techniques to make certain their realistic implementation and adoption. This consists of imparting schooling and belongings to group individuals to make sure they will be familiar with the checklist and its utilization.

Customization for unique industries and professions: Checklists want to be tailored to the unique dreams and requirements of numerous industries, professions, or non-public goals. Customization makes the checklists greater relevant, realistic, and powerful in their application.

Measurement and evaluation: The effectiveness of checklists must be measured and evaluated via relevant metrics and facts. This enables in figuring out areas of development and optimizing the checklists for better effects.

Learn from real-international case research: Real-worldwide case studies provide precious insights and examples of a fulfillment tick list implementation. Studying such case research can provide precious commands and concept for enforcing checklists in one among a type settings.

Finally, Checklists have proven to be effective equipment for enhancing productiveness, improving accuracy, and optimizing consequences in numerous fields, industries, and elements of each day existence. Real-global case studies provide compelling evidence of a success tick list implementation and offer treasured lessons at the advantages and annoying conditions of incorporating checklists into distinct workflows, strategies, and professions. By embracing the commands located from the ones case research and implementing checklists efficiently, people and groups can gain superior productiveness, accuracy, and results in their respective domain names.

Chapter 17: What Is Consistency?

Consistency is conformity in making use of some factor, usually required for the sake of not unusual sense, accuracy, or equity."

That is the most complete definition of consistency. When you study it that manner, it appears very primary and clean to put into impact on your lifestyles. It seems clean to be constant and rely entirely on and amplify near constant humans. But slowly. It's extra complex than you may recollect.

Far too many people recollect that being in reality ordinary is probably smooth. They trust it's going to probable be easy to enforce this idea and make it a regular part of their lives. I may be a ordinary person without hassle, and as quickly as I begin, I'll in no way quit, they guarantee themselves. Yet that is simply no longer the case.

Give Credit to Consistency

The truth is that greater humans need to fee consistency. But, irrespective of being not noted and undervalued as a key life method, consistency has helped many people thrive and might do the equal for you.

So, what precisely is consistency? Not the definition or the hazy description we provided earlier. What does real consistency appearance and revel in like in real existence? And what's the end result? What are some real examples of consistency?

Let us begin with what consistency isn't always. Being constant does not imply giving in or persisting in a role bad to you, your courting, your profession, or others. That does not recommend you need to study preceding rituals or mind in the present generation due to the truth topics are converting quicker than inside the beyond.

No, preserving continuity does no longer require refusing to regulate to changing times. Far too many humans in the global are continuously inconsistent in all the incorrect strategies. Consistency does no longer recommend

You can be nasty or hurtful to others, even in case you do now not know or apprehend them. That isn't being constant or "actual to oneself," but as an alternative merciless.

Doing what continuously works necessitates consistency in each philosophy and exercise. It approach sticking to tried-and-real processes that get the manner finished, regardless of the paintings. When what you're doing is operating, there may be no purpose to alternate in reality due to the fact the contemporary politician, industrial business enterprise multi-millionaire, or life teach says you need to. It's approximately cutting thru the distractions and temptations of get-it-accomplished-quick plans and techniques and doing what works and guarantees the outstanding effects time and time all over again.

When you take a look at someone's success in employer, it's no longer commonly due to the reality they were seeking to shake things up, suppose outdoor the sector, and do some factor completely particular. Most of the time, the ones billionaires and worldwide-elegance professionals succeed with the aid of manner of doing what works. They hold subjects easy, hold their eyes at the prize, discover a way to achieve what they want, and preserve on with it. It is the definition of consistency. Throughout records, it has helped many people gain great achievement.

Maintain Consistency

Another part of consistency is staying regular and reliable. To see effects, you want to located within the persistent strive. It applies to all aspects of your life, which include your professional, non-public, and social lives. For instance, going to the health club three instances in line with week is a ways superior to operating out difficult every day and ultimately carrying out in case you're looking for to get in form. Putting up the try might assist, and the effects will take a look at. There is not any way spherical it.

It is an critical element of consistency: you're best now and again doing it for others. Perhaps you're handiest being consistent with yourself. Being real to your self refers to a variety of things. For example, it consists of sticking to a food regimen and treating your body properly, going to mattress at a normal hour, continuing to touch and be close to the people you need, and every now and then treating yourself.

When you start to be ordinary on this area of your existence, not simplest with others however moreover with your self, you may live a happier, more worthwhile life.

What are a few appropriate strategies for bringing consistency into your lifestyles? Consider losing weight. Do you agree with you studied it's far higher to devour all the time healthily with occasional sweet treats carefully? It outcomes in slower but longer-lasting weight reduction or going on a series of dramatic crash diets discovered thru binges.

Knowing what consistency is and then taking a step lower lower again to determine out a way to exercising it within the real international, for your self and others, is step one in the direction of becoming regular. Now that we comprehend what consistency is, allow's communicate approximately why it's miles essential, what it method, and the manner you could exercising small things time and again to grow to be greater ordinary.

Chapter 18: Why Is Consistency Important?

What is it about consistency that makes it so vital in each your private and expert life? There are numerous reasons inside the lower returned of this. As you have were given a examine consistency cautiously, you may discover how it can gain you in plenty of regions.

In a international wherein we want strength of will and strength of thoughts to interest on what's essential to us, consistency can help us reduce thru the noise. Yet, to construct a nicely designed addiction, you need to be disciplined. And this discipline continues you from straying from your course. It is the primary cause why consistency is so crucial.

Life And Business Consistency

Assume you are attempting to set up a modern-day enterprise or net presence. If that is the case, you may need to be self-disciplined to create some thing as a manner to thrive and persist for a long term.

Create a way that will help you live targeted, discover new fabric, write the object's outline and frame, and edit and submit it. And you must do it all over again the subsequent week. It advantages you, your writing, your abilities, and your selected goal market.

Would you watch a TV display that failed to air frequently? Would you purchase a newspaper which you didn't supply each day?

It will take paintings. Nothing, however, that calls for willpower, self-discipline, and an entire lot of attempt is simple. In the end, you may see the results.

With a few consistency, you may moreover experience higher approximately yourself. There is a few other reason why you have to encompass it in your life. If you continuously observe via on your commitments, you'll have more self perception in your self, and others can also have extra faith in you.

Developing the particular task, you're operating on every day may make you experience extra assured and satisfied with your desires. As a end give up end result, you'll hold to paintings tough, create greater, and advantage more success.

To be regular, it isn't always about the final results or the give up line. The development you make on every occasion you construct that one-of-a-kind enterprise is what consistency is all approximately.

You can adventure lower back in time and study the way you finished this morning, or 3 weeks within the beyond. It is prepared the manner and growth, now not the results. You can modify your velocity with the aid of reading your improvement, gaining a large sense of your sources, and maintaining a easy and unique approach.

You may additionally moreover additionally beautify yourself-self guarantee and get more comfortable with intention-setting with the aid of retaining song of your progress.

Everything Consistency Can Bring You

Do you need to face out from the organization? Be honest. Do you need to be placed? Be honest. Show up on time, every time, each day. If you could set up yourself as a dependable and regular individual, creator, or businessperson, you'll without a doubt benefit a following and connections with the humans that rely number.

Create some detail worth talking approximately or promoting. Only some belongings you placed out there'll pass viral. Only a few corporation ventures will garner the attention and fans you attempting to find. Only some relationships may be prolonged-term ones. On the alternative hand, being there every day will collect human beings's take delivery of as actual with and preserve their hobby. Because over time, the ones small, clear-cut movements will upload as tons as large consequences for yourself, your friends and circle of relatives, the institutions you begin, and how you view your self and the area see you.

Maintaining our commitment to difficult art work may also help us succeed distinctly.

When you behave regularly, you adopt the identical things almost every day. When we fail to finish duties for a day or and in the long run fail to achieve our reason, it is straightforward to recognize why. Consistency holds us answerable for all of our moves.

No one else is accountable if you carry out the responsibilities required to obtain your desires. We may additionally moreover want to revise our plans.

Because we can pass over one or workdays, we must engage in sports activities and increase conduct to complete our plans.

Consistency in each day life assists us in turning into more sincere inside the eyes of others. Preaching to others is easy, however embodying our necessities may be more hard. Others see individuals who "walk the stroll" as fairly sincere and dependable. When others accept as true with in you, it boosts your self guarantee and verifies that what you are doing is absolutely really worth. Other people's religion in us boosts our self perception and gives us with the motivation to preserve running within the path of all of our desires.

Regarding don't forget, your steady standard overall performance can growth our relevance and reputation, in particular in case you art work in a organization or are a leader in a few manner. People want to art work with humans with a installed track document of fulfillment due to the fact steady hard paintings produces lengthy-term effects. It ought to bring about new consumer possibilities in the destiny. Working tough and constantly can notably effect whether you're promoted or stay a rank-and-report worker.

Self-manage is vital.

Being constant may be difficult as it calls for a whole lot of electricity of will, and if one isn't always used to retaining consistent in a single's activities, it can turn out to be a present day addiction. Consistent practice strengthens trouble, sharpens our interest, and heightens our reputation of what should be done. It is probably difficult to interrupt antique behavior, however consistency in our paintings is needed to perform higher and experience private boom.

After time and again operating toward a brand new know-how, you may decide whether or now not or no longer it's going to be triumphant or fail. If obtaining outcomes is your element, you could prevent doing some factor or give up in case you do no longer see at once outcomes. If you're advocated to perform subjects frequently, you could push via and compare whether or not or now not they may obtain success.

For all you apprehend, a assignment can also most effective require minimal adjustments to the technique to succeed, and you can only understand in case you live with it earlier than giving up.

Chapter 19: Why You Shouldn't Think Of Consistency As All Or Nothing

Regardless of the proof and records, many believe they may be both splendid successes or horrible failures. Many human beings ought to recognize what they have completed, in spite of the truth that it is incredible and worthy of glory and acclaim.

Others don't forget they have got finished more than enough and do not want to hold, strive tougher, or acquire something more.

It is a case of all-or-now not some thing thinking. It's the notion that it is both this or that, A or B, and now not some thing else. When you live a existence of all black-and-white thinking with out a gray, you do yourself a huge disservice and critically restrict your capability.

Many people adhere to black-and-white, all-or-now not some thing wondering even as attempting to be everyday. Why is it the type of ordinary function of folks seeking to add more balance? It's uncertain, however it has some issue to do with the fact that it hurts to appearance your self installation dreams after which fall brief of them. Both constantly and in no manner

This manner of questioning can motive many troubles, mainly in case you're seeking to be everyday and dependable. All-or-not anything questioning influences the manner you perceive your self and others. Absolute terms like "usually" or "in no manner" are often used in this mode of questioning. "I'll never continuously be ordinary, so I should now not try!" It is some aspect that many humans tell themselves as they attempt to be extra constant of their non-public and expert lifestyles. Furthermore, many human beings can't see alternate opportunities because of the reality there may be without a doubt appropriate or evil, with out a in-between. That also can make finding answers hard, if no longer not possible.

When you observe all-or-no longer something wondering, you can often sense like a failure.

You may additionally have decrease vanity because whilst you're both a success or a failure - and no longer anything else - the chances of appearing to be a entire failure are extensively higher.

You can also be an entire lot a good deal less organized to take dangers when you have an all-or-now not something mind-set, making it hard to be constant regularly. It might assist if you took positive possibilities to convert your life and the way you do topics, which include the way you will be regular, honest, and reliable. You need to think outdoor the sphere, take a look at with new subjects, push yourself, and blend topics up. But you can't do that often if you count on in phrases of all or now not whatever.

Also, you will find it tough to forgive your self regularly, so all-or-not something wondering can not be used on the equal time as becoming a constant character. When you don't meet the ultra-modern necessities you have set for your self, you want to be patient with yourself. It would help if you informed yourself that on the equal time as you possibly did not whole all your dreams, you in all likelihood did attempt, that's something to be thrilled with. That is a reason to have a first-rate time. You can not get once more on the pony and try another time in case you cannot forgive your self. And that is a important trouble of turning into steady or wearing out something else.

Indeed, grace, self-forgiveness, and self-compassion are required to boom yourself and grow to be a higher character.

A sympathetic character. And considering all or now not something will not will let you achieve this.

When someone thinks in this fashion, they'll only think about themselves as a success or failing in their lifestyles pastimes. It's all black and white; it's far both this or that. That is the middle of all-or-no longer something questioning, and it is able to take you down a path from which you can not go back. It's a Struggle

Becoming everyday can be tough. You need to set a purpose for your self and bring together a vision of the version of your self that you want to be. Then it is a count range of following through and taking the measures required to emerge as that man or woman. That is an giant mission! That way you are not in all likelihood to be exceptional all the time.

You will make errors, fall short, and need to observe, try all over again, and regulate your technique to consistency. And in case you assume in terms of all or no longer something, black and white, you may constantly restrict yourself.

This manner of thinking is probably higher whilst in search of to be ordinary, but it's also elaborate while constructing relationships with others. You examine your worthiness as both top or terrible. Yet, with this binary intellectual pattern, you may begin to revel in unique folks. As a end result, you could pass harsh and unfair judgment on your self and others. When you're so pessimistic, the vicinity can seem like a totally bleak location, reinforcing your feelings of cynicism, despair, and worry.

You can also additionally additionally preference consistency not best from your self but also from others. That approach you may assume masses from others in your life. You will want them to be dependable and easy. Nevertheless, as formerly said, doing so is first-rate sometimes sincere. You are not on my own in making mistakes and falling short from time to time. Others will only every so often be able to gain consistency over time. It would require time, fake beginnings, revisions, and frustrating moments.

If you continue to be all or now not anything, you can not permit the ones near you to try, fail, strive again, and in the end achieve success. It will now not permit you or others close to you to be regular.

The critical truth is that suffering from all-or-no longer some thing questioning will not benefit you. It will handiest serve to set unjust requirements for your self and others. That is a specific method to restrict yourself and assure that you'll in no way change and that the changes made through using others might be inadequate for you.

As you can see, it need to be averted - especially if you are striving to make a sizable exchange for your existence, inclusive of becoming greater honest.

Chapter 20: How Little Actions Can Lead To Great Results

As with maximum subjects, turning into a ordinary individual is a marathon, no longer a dash.

You've possibly heard that before about tremendous subjects, however it's miles though proper for consistency. Suppose you need to grow to be a honest character or run a dependable commercial business enterprise. In that case, you could expect to preserve your mindset at the vicinity, how you do business enterprise, and the manner you supply your self and live your lifestyles overnight.

That is, of path, an all-or-no longer something manner of wondering. And, as formerly stated, being in that mindset will slow you down or prevent you from being steady.

The fact is that turning into a consistent person may be hard at the start. You can also moreover persuade yourself that you have been a nice way your entire life and that converting that now could require massive alternate.

Allow Plenty of Time

You may want to require quite a few strive, however right proper here's the detail: this artwork may be finished at a time. You can do it step by step but step by step over time. As complicated as it may sound, turning into steady is an act of consistency.

Instead of trying to undergo a sea change and substantially redecorate your lifestyles all at once, use the marathon analogy and start adjusting small topics proper right here and there over the years. Before you realize it, you may change your entire life and the way you manage your commercial organization and personal affairs, and you can understand which you have end up the kind of individual you continuously knew you'll be - you in all likelihood did no longer do it unexpectedly.

Little steps are what you require. What are some easy actions you may take to come to be and live ordinary?

Developing a nighttime ritual that you can accomplish every day is a extraordinary idea. That's commonly a pleasant location to start. Why overdue at night time? Putting too much stress on oneself inside the morning can be too much. You have already got a brilliant deal to do in the morning, so cope with the middle of the night.

Perhaps you are looking to test a book. Here's an amazing first step you may take: Before going to bed, I test three pages. Set aside 15 minutes, no matter what, to take a look at those three pages. You will look at your 3 pages no matter what you have were given completed inside the course of the day, while you want to awaken or how exhausted you are. It's only 3! That is some issue you may do quick! You will advantage this every night time time.

That would possibly not even need to be some thing as massive as that. It's as easy as utilising moisturizer to your toes earlier than bed. That's a simple movement you can take every night. It high-quality takes some seconds.

Whatever it is, you have to do it every night. It is the gadget of establishing consistency. Purposefully being everyday and proving to your self that you may accomplish that. You are demonstrating to yourself that you may accomplish consistency, although it's a ways with some thing minor. It can are available in to be had while you experience like you've got taken on more than you could bite. You'll appearance again on those modest steps and recollect that you can do it. Why? Because you have got got have been given, and this can characteristic evidence.

Compile the Minor Details

The secret to turning into consistent is to take all the minor belongings you do often and bring together them proper right into a story you inform yourself. You will see that you in the meantime are simply consistent while you upload those small information. You have not advised yourself, "I want to acquire 15 mins early each day with out fail." Instead, you stated, "I want to evoke 5 minutes earlier every day," "I want to preserve a snack to art work every day," and "I want to begin my vehicle ten mins in advance."

These are all little levels and dreams that you can accomplish. When you add them all collectively, you get conventional fulfillment.

As you could see, taking modest actions consequences in huge results. You first rate want to decide your selected result and then choose out the modest moves you may take to get there. There is not this kind of thing as too many modest steps. When you located all of them collectively, they screen a path that in the end ends in the man or woman you need to be and the consistency you want to expose off.

Chapter 21: How To Keep Being Consistent

You now understand the way to be consistent, but the most essential difficulty of consistency is retaining steady. And it can be greater complicated than you think.

Indeed, if you begin to be everyday however then drop the ball and save you, you may be squandering a while and others. The complete intention of consistency is to stay constant.

But how do you pass approximately doing that? How do you keep going? How are you capable of avoid dropping the ball? It's pretty easy, but it does require a few forethought and attempt. Yet it is properly properly well worth the attempt in the end.

Here are some activities and keep in thoughts if you want to preserve your beautiful success.

Be Realistic in Your Goals: It might be simpler to be everyday if you understand what to do. Keep it easy,

As a give up end result, the desires are unambiguous and clean to show display. You may additionally want to begin thru sketching out your definition of consistency. Secondly, bear in mind the minor steps you need to take to attain that purpose. As formerly indicated, this could hold you ordinary and save you your assignment from turning into too big, overwhelming, or no longer possible.

Sustain Consistency: Maintaining consistency necessitates knowledge what desires to be performed every day. As a end end result, you ought to plan a way for your self. Whether it's miles an organizer, a now not, or a list of notifications on your cellular phone, this could help you preserve prepared. You can then decide which responsibilities you've got time for and that you do now not.

Employ Reminders: Because that is a brand new exercising, it's far critical to remind oneself to carry out it. Place reminders in your clothing, domestic, art work, and college. Fresh responsibilities and conversations are easy to overlook, specially even as on the lookout for to shake up your everyday. Put reminders in places wherein you may be conscious them so you will recollect them finally of the day.

You will make mistakes, no matter how hard you try to be normal. Thus, even in case you make mistakes, try to persevere. Even if you are well-prepared, you may make errors from time to time. As a prevent end result, you want to base your plans on your mistakes. If you're making a mistake, try not to criticize your self. Something like this occurs frequently.

If you break a promise, omit a date, or have to reschedule someone, you are not constantly losing consistency. Other factors may additionally moreover come into play. While getting prepared for the ones out of doors influences and seeking to keep away from them is crucial, they'll now and again derail us.

If you want to, you need to be extra regular. As a stop end end result, you need to get nicely sufficient sleep at night. An average grownup goals seven to eight hours of sleep in line with night time time. Those who are nonetheless in college are expected to do lots more. Allowing your frame time to get better will make retaining consistency the following day less complex.

Even if you need to look results proper now, it's going to take time. It can be hard to exchange your manner of thinking, and

There might be no at once repercussions. It may be no longer clean to uproot your whole existence and introduce a slew of latest practices simultaneously. It should help if you gave yourself time to decide what abilties superb for you.

It must help if you additionally had been tenacious even as maintaining sensible. Becoming a dependancy necessitates doing a little aspect regularly for round a month. Remember to set minor desires along the way. Try now not to cope with too much without delay. Little tweaks will upload up over time.

You'll additionally want to set obstacles in your intimate relationships and obligations. These boundaries make it less complicated so you can preserve half of of the agreement because of your expectations of others. Establishing those barriers will make certain you first-rate tackle what you can deal with. For example, inform your employer which you preference to artwork on some thing apart from weekends or at uncommon hours. You can also transfer your mobile cellphone off to notify your personnel that you may be unavailable on nights, weekends, or vacations.

If you convert your way of questioning, you may be extra normal. Remember this as you are on the lookout for for to trade a big detail of your existence.

Because we are not machines, there may be days while we do no longer experience like doing whatever. For this cause, we ought to all hire motivational gear. What ought to you do in case you lack the pressure to complete your art work? Even despite the fact that it is able to be tempting to desolate tract our dreams for the day, there are steps we are able to take to deal with this hassle. If you revel in down, lethargic, weary, or sad, you could attempt a few techniques to decorate your motivation.

Look after Yourself: Setting handiest commitments you can preserve is each different essential dependancy to boom in case you need to be extra ordinary. People adore it whilst others love them. As a result, at the same time as a person pleads for our help, all of us typically will be inclined to mention positive. While it's miles right to have the guide of others, it's far important to refrain from making guarantees we can not preserve.

Chapter 22: Habits And Consistency

Changing your behavior separately, little by little, is all it takes to end up extra regular.

When expressed this manner, it sounds a long manner too simplistic and as even though it might no longer do the folks who transformed sufficient justice. But this is the most purpose at the identical time as attempting to turn out to be constant. You need to end up aware of the behaviors you want to change or consist of into your routine and then pursue them.

Habits most effective final good-bye earlier than they grow to be a part of you. As you begin forcing your self to comply with those behavior, you will train your self to do them constantly and purpose them to part of your man or woman, lifestyles, and normal.

It is an vital detail of becoming regular however additionally a difficult difficulty. Forming new conduct is difficult, and retaining your self sincere and committed to repeating them is even greater hard.

Nonetheless, it's miles a vital step if you need to be normal and dependable.

Alter Your Habits

So, how are you going to shape new behavior and combine them into your persona?

It's quite sincere. To start, write a list of methods you desire to behave and the way you will be consistent. You'd want to enhance your reaction time to cellphone calls and emails. You may also want to achieve to paintings earlier. You need to visit the gymnasium regularly. You can also moreover pick out to prepare dinner at home in place of eating out.

Well, your dreams and the way you need your existence to seem. The 2nd step in this technique is to jot down down down the conduct so as to lead you to that place and help you purchased your desires. As formerly said, you may start small and increase behavior for your self.

If you want to enhance your phone call go back fee, you want to name a pal or member of the family at least as quick as in step with week, each week. If you want to obtain at artwork early, you can begin doing it as soon as every week however step by step growth your frequency.

I'll do it as soon as each week. The same holds for going to the gym or consuming at home.

Habits are frequently subjects that form organically inner us without the help of outdoor stimuli. So forcing oneself to make some also can sound bizarre. But remember what you may benefit in case you put in force the ones practices. It is the only approach to "train" your self the manner to carry out those duties and to do them often.

Chapter 23: What Benefits Can Consistency Provide You?

The best manner to determine what consistency can offer for you is to don't forget the way you revel in about ordinary human beings and businesses.

What involves mind even as you recall a person dependable and truthful, who's continually on time and usually presents what they promise, and who is in no way reminded or forced to do subjects? What are your thoughts about this person or business organization? Is it incredible or terrible? Is this a person you need to collaborate with frequently or avoid?

We presume which you value a person who is proper at their artwork, steady, and reliable. That is the affect human beings would probable have of you in case you artwork hard to come to be ordinary.

If you discern difficult to live regular, you may create a lifestyles complete of healthy, strong relationships, stable organisation connections, possibilities, exciting sports, and a serene and laid-yet again mood in the good deal.

Alter Your "YOU" Point of Perspective

The most vital thing that consistency can give you is how human beings understand you, their reviews, and their willingness to be with you and art work alongside you.

No one wants to paintings with or be close to a person who will constantly drop the ball and permit them to down. How often do you concentrate people talk kindly approximately folks that are erratic and untrustworthy? Not too regularly. It's absolutely one in each of a person's worst traits, and it is able to shatter relationships. That can leave you with few pals and no future industrial organisation possibilities.

You are pronouncing a few component whilst you're regular and dependable. You are virtually expressing state of affairs. You recommend being attentive to others, understanding their feelings, and respecting them. You suggest that their time is valuable and that you do now not take them, their time, or their availability for granted. That speaks volumes! That demonstrates which you are a loving, actual, and sympathetic man or woman. That is the sort of man or woman with whom others desire to be buddies.

When you are inconsistent, you are maintaining the complete opposite. You are implying that you realise someone is preoccupied or has asked some component of you, and you do not care. You'll do it even as you get to it, arrive at the equal time as you need to, and do the whole thing at your private tempo. It isn't someone who makes concessions, listens to others, or in fact cares approximately their sentiments.

www.ingramcontent.com/pod-product-compliance
Lightning Source LLC
Chambersburg PA
CBHW071440080526
44587CB00014B/1930